"Health begins with what's on your plate. But 'wellness' is *alchemy*—an elusive and delicate ballet of body, mind, and spirit ever striving for perfect harmony. Deftly leveraging the wisdom and experience of the world's greatest wellness experts, *Wellth* is a brilliantly composed, highly engaging memoir and easy-to-digest primer on exactly how you, too, can be healthy and happy, live your best life, and thrive. A must read!"

—Rich Roll, wellness advocate and bestselling author of *Finding Ultra* and *The Plantpower Way*

"I love Jason's work and his first book is a personal, smart, and informative read. *Wellth* shares his deep wisdom and helps you enjoy a more exciting, energized, healthy, and ultimately well-lived life."

—Dan Buettner, National Geographic fellow and *New York Times* bestselling auth͟   ͟ ͟he Blue Zones Solution

"*Wellth* reminds us ͭ   ͦwn, having gratitude, and pla ͨ   can and do have
truly abunda   ͭta, actress and supermodel

"*Wellth* is a folksy ͙mulation of what we need to know about living a rich and fulfilling life. Written in a humble, trustworthy voice, complex and often contradictory knowledge is made accessible and clear."

—Frederic Luskin, Ph.D., director of the Stanford Forgiveness Project

"I wish all my patients and readers would grab a copy of *Wellth*. To truly thrive, we all need what Jason Wachob shares with us here. More wellth, not wealth. It's that simple and that important."

—Mark Hyman, M.D., director at the Cleveland Clinic Center for Functional Medicine and author of #1 *New York Times* bestseller *The Blood Sugar Solution*

"For a comprehensive yet simple guide on how to live a healthier life, look no further. *Wellth,* a new book by mindbodygreen founder Jason Wachob, takes a holistic approach to happiness, success, and wellness. Mr. Wachob gives new currency to mental, physical, and emotional well-being. The advice in *Wellth* is firsthand: a Wall Street expatriate's personal accounts. Refreshingly sincere and engaging, readers are humbled, surprised, and invigorated. Be prepared to shed a tear, start yoga, question your doctor's advice, and eat more vegetables."

—*New York Observer*

"Jason Wachob's book reminds the global community to shift our goals from material possessions to love, happiness, joy, and purpose. By sharing his engaging personal stories of trials and growth, we gain a refreshing perspective on what to do to ensure our own well-being."

—Tara Stiles, founder of Strala Yoga

"An easy and great read for anyone who is a reticent convert to living a little better (specifically guys who resist kale)."

—*Goop*

Wellth

*How to Build a Life,
Not a Résumé*

JASON WACHOB

Founder and CEO of mindbodygreen

HARMONY

BOOKS · NEW YORK

Originally published in hardcover in the United States by
Harmony Books, an imprint of the Crown Publishing Group,
a division of Penguin Random House LLC, New York, in 2016.

This work was inspired by the author's blog,
"39 Life Lessons I've Learned in 39 Years."

Library of Congress Cataloging-in-Publication Data
Names: Wachob, Jason.
Title: Wellth / Jason Wachob.
Description: New York : Harmony, [2016]
Identifiers: LCCN 2015028567 | ISBN 9781101904480 (hardback)
Subjects: LCSH: Nutrition. | Health. | Food. | BISAC: SELF-HELP /
Personal Growth / Happiness. |SELF-HELP / Personal Growth / Success.
|BIOGRAPHY & AUTOBIOGRAPHY / General.
Classification: LCC RA784 .W216 2016 | DDC 613.2—dc23 LC record
available at https://protect-us.mimecast.com/s/RKomBxS7QKATQ

ISBN 978-1-101-90450-3
eBook ISBN 978-1-101-90449-7

PRINTED IN THE UNITED STATES OF AMERICA

Book design by Anna Thompson
Cover design by Jennifer Carrow
Cover photographs: (sunglasses) ARZTSAMUI/Moment Open/Getty Images;
(landscape) Primeimages/E+/Getty Images

10 9 8 7 6 5 4 3 2 1

First Paperback Edition

*Behind every great man there's a great woman,
and for me there are three: to my mother,
who always told me I could accomplish anything;
to my grandmother looking down from above;
and to the love of my life, my wife, Colleen.*

CONTENTS

INTRODUCTION   3

1. Eat   8

2. Move   22

3. Work   36

4. Believe   60

5. Explore   84

6. Breathe   102

7. Feel   116

8. Love   136

9. Heal   158

10. Thank   178

11. Ground   194

12. Live   208

13. Laugh   224

ACKNOWLEDGMENTS   229

NOTES   231

INDEX   237

Wellth

WEALTH

*noun | \welth\ Derived from the Middle English, welthe:
meaning well-being and happiness*

: a large amount of money and possessions

WELLTH

noun | \welth\ A new and more valuable life currency

*: a life exemplified by abundance, happiness, purpose,
health, and joy.*

INTRODUCTION

DON'T GET ME WRONG. I like money. But there's more to life. Many of us aren't satisfied with just trying to grow our bank accounts so we can spend our hard-earned cash on nice, shiny things. The good life is no longer just about the material—instead, it can be found in a lifestyle that is devoted to mental, physical, spiritual, and emotional health. Along with that is the ability to feel happy and comfortable in one's own skin. While many people would include being "wealthy" when defining a good life, I believe that it's time to return to the original definition.

I came up with another word, *wellthy*, to further emphasize the importance of well-being to you (*thy*) and to us all. A wellthy existence is one in which happiness is attainable, health is paramount, and daily living is about abundance. It's a life in which work is purposeful; friendships are deep and plentiful; and there's a daily sense of richness or overflowing joy. But since there's no one-size-fits-all definition for a wellthy existence, I hope this book will serve as a guide to help you embark on your own personal journey that is both unique and meaningful.

The first wealth is health.

—RALPH WALDO EMERSON, *CONDUCT OF LIFE*

Like you, I'm on a search for a balanced, fulfilling life. I'm not a doctor or a healer. I'm not a professional athlete or a celebrity. I'm not a billionaire, and I didn't come up from abject poverty. I have many lessons to share, but I'm not a life coach. And although I've been to a therapist, I'm certainly not one. Instead, I'm a regular person who, because of my work in the wellness community—in particular through my website, mindbodygreen.com—happens to know some of the most insightful health and wellness experts in the world. You will meet some of them in these pages, including yoga instructor Kathryn Budig, meditation teacher Charlie Knoles, functional medicine pioneer Dr. Frank Lipman, and relationship expert Dr. Sue Johnson, among others.

I've learned a lot from these experts and from my own challenging and magical life experiences. At age forty-one, I've finally achieved some of the most important aspects of a wellthy life—having control of my monkey mind, or overactive mental state; being at ease in my body; maintaining a daily sense of balance; having meaningful relationships; and experiencing an overall feeling of abundance and well-being (at least most of the time). I'm blessed to have a life and work that are aligned with my values, and a vibrant community that supports me.

Don't get me wrong. Although I have accomplished some of my dreams, I'm certainly not perfect—far from it. I found out the hard way that Wall Street can leave you empty; that death can change your life, yoga can save your life, and work is meaningful only when it truly aligns with your values. I've had plenty of failures, and I know that I will continue to make monumental mistakes. But I've had an interesting journey, and I hope that you'll be entertained by and relate to my adventures. I was a happy-go-lucky, heavy-drinking frat boy and then a successful trader, who gave it all up to become a wellness entrepreneur. I've gone from being flat broke and depressed to being enlivened by a mission and then raising the capital to pursue it. I spent three years working on mindbodygreen.com in a tiny apartment while my wife supported me. We've gone from zero to 15 million unique viewers per month and it's now a leading media brand in wellness.

Before mindbodygreen.com launched, phrases like *mind-body spirit*, *mind-body soul*, and *mind-body connection* were all pretty common. So why did I call the website mindbodygreen, which wasn't part of the lexicon at that time? And why is *mindbodygreen* one word and not three?

Whether we like it or not, everything is connected: our minds, our bodies, and our environment. The mind and body are not separate; they're one. That's why we could read every book in the self-help section, and follow someone else's rigid rules, but still not have wellth. If we're out of touch with the mind or the body, then we're not truly healthy because we're disconnected from the self. And as you'll see in the "Ground" chapter, the green aspect of wellth is crucial, too. As a city dweller, I've even found it incredibly important to connect to nature, and that it's impossible to live in a healthy manner if we aren't aware of the impact of toxins and chemicals on our minds, our bodies, and our environment.

Along with the mindbodygreen experts, I will lead you through the steps to true wellth, starting with the basic physical areas (eat, move), then going to how we earn a living (work); from the way our thoughts shape our experiences (believe), to the importance of finding our flow and passion (explore). Then together we'll look at the need for a mind-body practice (breathe) and the importance of having friends and a good support system to our emotional health (feel). But you can't be wellthy if your relationships are in ruin—those with others as well as the closest relationship you'll ever have: your relationship to yourself. So we explore relationships (love), taking care of our bodies when things go off-track (heal), the importance of gratitude (thank), and how an intimate connection to the earth and nature sustains us (ground). Then I discuss dealing with the most natural of human circumstances, death and grief, and how the knowledge that we all eventually die can inform the way we live. I close the book with a chapter on laughter, because if you can't enjoy yourself, then what's the point?

It's my hope that you, too, can flourish in all aspects of your life. What follows will give you lots of ideas for investing in you and, in doing so, becoming truly wellthy.

CHAPTER 1

Eat

ONE OF THE FIRST AND most elemental aspects of accruing wellth comes from how we nourish our bodies. It seems that everyone wants to know the perfect "diet" in order to look great. Many think that means eating exclusively organic, vegetarian/vegan, raw, Paleo, low-fat, or low-carb foods. But how do you tell which eating plan is best for you? Is there a one-size-fits-all diet that leads to wellth?

When it comes to diets, I've tried them all. Every diet book you'll read promises benefits like weight loss, increased energy, glowing skin, better sex, and increased productivity and focus; but I believe that these one-size-fits-all approaches are all wrong. Yet I think there are a few universal truths.

I'm six foot seven, and I weigh 220 pounds. A third-degree sprain in my right ankle from twenty-five years ago still won't let me ground my heel onto the floor. I love playing basketball, but I've always hated running. Back in college, I could get my elbow above the rim and dunk very easily, but no more. I love Brussels sprouts but hate mushrooms. Oddly enough, I'm allergic to celery. Each and every one of us has our own physical gifts, quirks, likes, and dislikes. This may sound obvious, but sometimes it seems as if those in the health and diet industry think otherwise.

I'm not just talking about the health care system and the way doctors treat symptoms rather than patients. I'm referring to the way we think about everyday diet and exercise. How can one particular diet or workout be good for the entire world? How can a diet be the same for a six-foot-seven, 220-pound, forty-one-year-old man who practices fifteen minutes of yoga a few times a week; and a five-foot-two, 102-pound, twenty-two-year-old woman who runs fifteen miles every day? How can being vegan or Paleo be good for everyone? How can anyone believe that their health routine is appropriate for everyone else?

In reality, what is good for me may be awful for you. I absolutely love coffee, and I'm delighted that it has antioxidants that may fight cancer. But for my coworker, even a sip causes painful acid reflux. For him, it's green tea all the way. My wife loves running with the rising sun. I hate running at any time of day. Just the idea of getting dressed to go for a run triggers a stress response in my body.

To be truly wellthy is to find your personal prescription—to discover what works for you, what feels good, what you love. That process of discovery never ends. There are certain diets and types of exercise that are right for you in certain periods of your life but not others. Not only do we have to find the approach that works for us; we need to learn how to adapt that approach, or change it entirely, throughout our lives.

I was a gym rat for much of my twenties and early thirties, lifting weights and doing the elliptical machine daily. In my mid-thirties, after yoga played a huge role in healing my back,

I practiced yoga every morning and did nothing else. In my late thirties and now forties, I've switched it up again. Now I do yoga at home a few days a week for fifteen minutes, lift weights twice a week for 25 minutes, and meditate daily for twenty minutes.

As passionately as Paleo expert Chris Kresser advocates for his diet, he also teaches that our bodies need different diets and foods at different stages of our lives. Being an omnivore might be great for us at age twenty, but at age twenty-five, we might want to be vegetarian. At thirty, we might find that being vegan is just what the doctor ordered. At forty, we might try Paleo; and at age forty-five, go back to being an omnivore once again.

This has certainly been my experience. In my mid-twenties I thrived on a low-carb, low-sugar diet during the week, and on the weekends I ate and drank anything I wanted to. (I definitely did too much drinking!) In my mid-thirties, when I began to get serious about yoga, I felt better as a vegetarian, although occasionally I ate meat. My digestion improved when I went gluten-free. Then in my late thirties I went Paleo, eating a lot of cooked vegetables, grass-fed beef, wild salmon, and no raw foods (in an effort to kick a parasite). In the past few months, I went back again to eating mostly vegetables (cooked or raw), and I don't eat much red meat. I've added a variety of grains and the occasional gluten.

I discovered that it no longer serves me to resist going to Roberta's for the best pizza in Brooklyn once in a while. Pleasure is not to be underestimated. I'll also have a margarita or two (or three!) whenever I eat Mexican food—there's one that I love that is made of carrot juice! Sometimes we all need a doughnut. It's probably not a great idea to eat one every day, but the occasional treat isn't going to kill you. Life should be fun. Being obsessive about diet can be stressful and can bring on orthorexia—an *un*healthy obsession with healthy eating. So aim to be balanced in your eating, as well as in your life.

Someone has to stand up and say that the answer isn't another pill. The answer is spinach.

—BILL MAHER

And keep in mind that our diets and bodies change, so it's important to listen and fine-tune your diet whenever you sense that something may be off, whether it's digestive issues, a lack of energy, weight gain, or boredom and a lack of pleasure in your eating. Don't fall victim to health orthodoxy that gives you no room for experimentation. Tune in to what feels good. Be open to change. Our bodies are constantly shifting, and so should our personal approaches to wellness.

Yet I do think that my doctor friends all would agree that processed foods are not ideal. I try not to demonize entire food groups, but I'm okay with demonizing sugar. There are studies that go as far as saying that sugar is more addictive than cocaine. Oh, and that sugar is making us fat and sick, too. There's a great documentary film, *Fed Up,* that dives into some of the harsh realities of sugar. For example, did you know that 80 percent of the 600,000 items sold in grocery stores have added sugar? Or that a typical bottle of soda contains 16 teaspoons of sugar from high-fructose corn syrup? Did you ever notice that on all nutrition labels there's a "recommended daily percent" right next to calories, fat, protein—but there's no recommended percentage for sugar, although it's now being discussed by the FDA.

You can't expect to live a vibrant life when you live on Twinkie consciousness.

—KRIS CARR, WELLNESS ACTIVIST AND DOCUMENTARY FILMMAKER

Still not sold on the evils of sugar? Then you should watch the great April 2012 segment on *60 Minutes* titled "Cancer Loves Sugar." It explains that some of this country's most respected institutions have found that sugar can lead to chronic illnesses such as heart disease, obesity, and cancer.

There are so many different viewpoints about food that a routine trip to the grocery store can quickly turn into an episode of *Portlandia*. With labels like *low-fat, non-GMO, local, organic, natural, wild, grass-fed, cage-free, gluten-free,* and *dairy-free* (I could go on and on), merely shopping for dinner can be overwhelming. But a few straightforward suggestions can help to streamline the process.

Keep it simple. Try to avoid gluten, sugar, and processed foods whenever possible. If it's in a box and has a label, then try not to make a habit of buying it. Avoiding processed foods can seem almost impossible at first, but after a few weeks it becomes easier. Author and wellness expert Dr. Mark Hyman says, "Stick to things that God made and not that man made." Eat real food. Mostly shop the perimeter of the grocery store, and buy fresh vegetables and fruits. If you're buying red meat, then make sure it's grass-fed or at least antibiotic and hormone free. And if you're buying fish, make sure it's wild.

Diets Come and Go

THE DIET BUSINESS IS MONSTROUS. There's a diet for pretty much anything these days: low-fat, low-carb, gluten-free, sugar-free. However, diets come and go, but a lifestyle stays with you forever. (I'm going to jump into the ring with my idea for my next book, a diet called *Eat Mostly Vegetables*. The beauty of the book is that the title is also the entire contents. I have a feeling no one will publish it.)

Eat food. Not too much. Mostly plants.

—MICHAEL POLLAN, *IN DEFENSE OF FOOD*

Actually, I don't believe in diets per se, as opposed to general dietary guidelines. Instead, I choose to be mindful; that's my lifestyle when it comes to food. I want to know where my food comes from. I want to know if it was sprayed with chemicals or if any antibiotics were used on it. I want to know if it contains added sugar or gluten. I want to know if it was processed. And even though this is a tall order, I'd also like to know if the people who picked, harvested, and produced this food were paid fair wages.

I want to know all these things. Sure, sometimes it's impossible to find out this information, particularly when eating in a restaurant. So when I don't have all the facts, I want to be mindful that I'm making a choice. Sometimes I choose to eat doughnuts that are laden with sugar and gluten and processed in a plant, simply because they taste so good. And sometimes I get pure, albeit fleeting, joy from eating that delicious doughnut. But when I do make that choice, I want it to be me who has made that decision. And I want to be okay with it.

This magical, marvelous food on our plate, this sustenance we absorb, has a story to tell. It has a journey. It leaves a footprint. It leaves a legacy. To eat with reckless abandon, without conscience, without knowledge; folks, this ain't normal.

—JOEL SALATIN, *FOLKS, THIS AIN'T NORMAL: A FARMER'S ADVICE FOR HAPPIER HENS, HEALTHIER PEOPLE, AND A BETTER WORLD*

Life—and junk food—happens. Contradictory? No, I don't think so. People aren't machines, and so we can be inconsistent. Human? Absolutely, yes. How do I balance eating the occasional doughnut while at the same time believing that sugar is terrible? The key word in that last sentence is *balance*. Sugar should be a treat, not a habit. Treats are a part of finding balance, until they become habitual, and that is when mindfulness becomes mindlessness.

Whatever you choose to eat, be mindful about it, so you can fully enjoy your choices.

—— Grow Your Life Savings: Eat ——

HOW DO WE KNOW WHEN our approach to diet isn't working? Dr. Frank Lipman is one of my food gurus and is also my
doctor. He shared his thoughts on diet, which I have found
incredibly helpful as I continue to reassess what feels right in
my body.

—— FIVE SIGNS YOUR DIET ISN'T WORKING FOR —— YOU—AND FOUR WAYS TO FIX IT FAST

1. **You're tired and listless much of the day.** If you're fatigued
or lethargic much of the time and lean on caffeine and sugar
to prop yourself up, it's time to take a close look at what you're
eating. Chances are, your diet is too short on nutrients to support you the way it should; so instead of feeling vibrant, you're
exhausted and drained. When you're eating a clean, colorful,
healthy diet, the body is powered up and nourished by the nutrients you're taking in, which enable you to feel alert, clear-
headed, and energized enough to go about your day without
needing a stimulant jolt. My favorite energy foods: green veg-
etable juices, whey protein in smoothies, nuts, fruit, and a good-
sized protein-filled lunch.

2. **Your belly is misbehaving. A lot.** Bloating, gas, constipation,
IBS, indigestion, and other digestive ills that so many of us think

of as normal or routine are anything but. One of the major signs that a dietary change is in order is digestion that's off. You're likely eating foods that irritate your digestive system, leading to an imbalance in your gut flora, those bacterial good guys who live in your gut, help you to digest your food, produce vitamins, excrete toxins, regulate hormones, and generally keep everything moving in the right direction. These functions go off the rails when there are too many of the bad guys and not enough of the good guys, so it's essential to feed the good guys really nutritious food. The big bad guys thrive on gluten, alcohol, sugar, and carbonated drinks. The big good guys love fermented and high-fiber foods, including lots of leafy vegetables. Also, try chewing thoroughly and resting your digestive system for ten hours a day. (No eating for two hours before sleep.)

3. **Your moods are all over the map.** Food has an impact on your mood. If you often feel like you're on an emotional roller coaster, it may be your diet that's taking you for a ride. Eating a diet that's high in sugar, gluten, alcohol, caffeine, or other irritants can push your mood up and down throughout the day, leaving you depressed, irritated, and anxious, regardless of how else the day is going. When you're eating the right diet for you, managing your moods becomes a much smaller job because you'll be putting your body through fewer, if any, of those chemically induced highs and lows. Keep a balance of protein, good fats, and fiber.

4. **You have skin issues that are written all over your face or body.** What's going on internally is reflected externally,

specifically on your skin. So if you're besieged by breakouts, rashes, eczema, or other skin issues, you should definitely take a hard look at what you're putting into your body. I've seen many of my patients transform their skin by making simple dietary changes, such as cutting out gluten, dairy, sugar, or alcohol. In fact, glowing skin is usually one of the first benefits my patients experience when adopting a healthier diet. When you remove the foods that are irritating your insides and you heal your gut, your skin becomes an external reflection of health.

5. **You always feel as if you've "got something" or are a little off.** Eating foods that are damaging to your body can send your immune system into overdrive. Your gut's lining is extremely thin—it's just one cell thick—and damage to it can be extremely problematic. About 70 percent of your immune system is found in your digestive tract. When this lining is damaged or worn down by a poor diet, then large food particles, bacteria, and toxins, which would normally stay inside the gut, instead can wind up breaking through into the bloodstream, where the immune system must deal with them. If you're constantly feeling a bit under the weather, that's a sign that you aren't eating foods that are properly supporting your immune system. Try incorporating garlic, fermented foods, probiotics, vitamin D, and coconut oil into your daily diet.

THE FIX
---

1. **Try an elimination diet, and be your own irritant detective.** If you really want to find out which foods are irritating your body and undermining your health and vitality, start with an elimination diet. This means removing the most common allergens or irritants from your diet. At the top of the potential irritants list: sugar, gluten, corn, soy, dairy, and alcohol. When you remove all these foods and substances at once, the body usually can heal quickly, and most people feel significantly better within two weeks. If you remove these foods and you feel great, that's a sure sign your diet wasn't nourishing you properly before.

2. **Then reintroduce foods slowly.** After you complete an elimination diet, I suggest you reintroduce foods slowly, one at a time, to see what kind of reaction (if any) you have to each one. When you reintroduce a food, have a small portion of it to see how your body reacts. Give your body two to three days before reintroducing another food, then try reintroducing one, wait a couple of days, and so on.

3. **Keep a food journal to monitor what works—and what doesn't.** As you're reintroducing foods you've eliminated, make sure to keep a food journal. This practice can be extremely helpful when you're figuring out what type of diet will keep you feeling your best. Note how your body responds to the food you've eaten. Did it make you feel tired? Energized? Moody? Did it digest well, or did you feel bloated? Did you get a headache? Track the physical and emotional responses that arise, and jot down your observations about what works for you and makes you feel great.

4. **Shake up your diet—try new foods.** One of the most important things you can do on your personal health journey is to be open to trying new ways of eating. If you've always eaten a lot of grains and beans and stayed away from animal products and you're not feeling great, you might try experimenting with a diet that includes more high-quality animal products and fewer grains to find out how your body responds. Do you always start the day with cereal, yogurt, or pancakes? Try whipping up a breakfast shake instead. Look for meal recipes that contain lots of nourishing protein and superfoods, such as sprouts or salmon, and see how your body responds.

A QUICK DEPOSIT IN YOUR WELLTH ACCOUNT

- One size doesn't fit all, when it comes to diet. Each person is an individual with different nutritional needs. What works as an eating plan for your best friend may not work for you.
- Be mindful of every bite you put into your mouth. Eat slowly, and enjoy the flavor and texture of your foods. The

more slowly you eat, the more full you'll feel, and the more you'll enjoy your food.

- Don't beat yourself up when you slip and eat something that isn't very healthy. Enjoy it, and then remember that your total lifestyle is what counts.
- When in doubt, eat vegetables!

CHAPTER 2

Move

MOVEMENT IS AN ESSENTIAL PART of the wellth equation. We all know that we need exercise for our bodies to function properly and maintain health. But what kind of exercise, and how much per day or week? Some experts advise getting between thirty and fifty minutes of exercise daily, alternating between aerobics and resistance training. For many people, a combination of jogging and weight lifting is ideal. Others enjoy Cross-Fit, spinning, or high-intensity interval training (HIIT).

Yes, I wholeheartedly believe that you need to find something that you really enjoy doing, and for which you can consistently find time. But if you're looking for something to add to your routine, or if you're experiencing pain that keeps you from moving comfortably—or you're in need of a simple stress reliever—then yoga is your ticket to wellth. I can vouch for it from personal experience. If I had to pick only one way to exercise, I'd pick yoga in a heartbeat.

In 2009 the stock market was in free-fall, and I was frantically trying to find funding for the startup I had cofounded. I was in a state because Crummy Brothers Organic Cookies was in big trouble. We had a great product, but we were extremely undercapitalized. The company's future was up in the air, to say the least, and I was literally up in the air nonstop. I had flown over 125,000 miles that year, traveling to more than 150 Whole Foods Markets to hawk our delicious and healthy cookies. As it has a way of doing, stress manifested itself in the weakest part of my body, my lower back. An old basketball injury had led to occasional flare-ups, yet I'd always been able to muscle through the pain. But this was different. The combination of frequent flying (which is itself a form of compression) and my six-foot-seven body being squashed into a little seat caused two extruded disks to press on my sciatic nerve.

I began to experience excruciating pain on a daily basis. I could walk barely more than a block without practically keeling over in pain. At a certain point, I had to sit after walking only a few steps. Then even sitting for brief periods became excruciating, never mind for hours at a time. Soon my ability to travel and therefore my living were at stake. Bed was the only place I found relief. But even then I was stressed out, as I lay there each night obsessing about how little money I had and how my promising business was going down the tubes.

It is health that is real wealth and not pieces of gold and silver.
—MAHATMA GANDHI

I tried cortisone shots, which didn't work, and then I went to a surgeon who specialized in lower back pain. He recommended surgery. My gut said no, loudly. I still thought of myself as a college basketball, tough-it-out kind of guy. It wasn't that I viewed surgery as defeat; some of my greatest sports heroes had gone under the knife and had not only survived but gone on to great things. Yet this option just didn't feel right for me. My pain was extreme, but somehow surgery felt more so, and I dreaded the recovery time as well.

Intuitively, I felt there had to be another solution. And so I sought a second opinion. My heart sank when the second specialist also recommended surgery. Yet as he was about to leave the examining room, his back already turned, he said, "Yoga might help." That got my attention. Rather than being dismissive, as I would have been a few years before, I was curious. If this Western doctor was remotely open to this yoga idea, maybe there was something to it.

I had no interest in going to a yoga class, though. I couldn't see myself as one of those mat-toting yogis rushing to a slick studio at lunchtime. In retrospect, my attitude was in part due to my being intimidated by the impossible-looking poses I saw in magazines, and scared that I might make my pain worse by overdoing it. Instead, I found a physical therapist who taught me a few restorative poses especially designed for back pain. I started to practice them every morning at home. I didn't tell anyone, not because I was embarrassed but because I didn't really think much about it at the time. I just saw yoga as something I'd try and then see what happened. I decided to apply the same discipline I'd done in high school when I was determined to master free throws on the basketball court.

I practiced every morning and evening. Before I boarded a plane to sit in one of those torturous seats, I did my yoga poses in the airport waiting area. It must have been quite a sight, all six foot seven of me doing a cat-cow in my suit. Within weeks, I began to feel better. Gradually I added more basic poses, and within a couple of months, the shooting pain began to subside dramatically. Within six months, the pain was completely gone. Yoga was one hell of a powerful afterthought.

Soon I found myself wanting more. I started classes at Strala Yoga in Manhattan after meeting the owners, Tara Stiles and her husband, Michael Taylor. They seemed down to earth and decidedly unintimidating. I loved their focus on movement and breath rather than nailing specific poses. Soon Tara's "Relax" class became my favorite. I had become one of those mat-toting yogis after all.

Health is a state of complete harmony of the body, mind and spirit. When one is free from physical disabilities and mental distractions, the gates of the soul open.

—B. K. S. IYENGAR, *YOGA: THE PATH TO HOLISTIC HEALTH*

As my yoga practice grew stronger, I found myself at Strala almost every day. Then I started to explore other studios and gravitated toward the more athletic Vinyasa flow style of yoga. It had a fast pace that felt really good. I still loved Tara's class and Vinyasa flow, but also enjoyed Kathryn Budig's class, where we'd learn how to turn upside down by doing headstands, forearm stands, or handstands (I never became a huge fan of these inversions, but they were fun to try); and I explored yoga classes all over the city, as I wanted to experience as many teachers and styles as possible. Some folks become wedded to one form of yoga—Vinyasa flow (which tends to be more athletic and "flows" from one pose to the next), Ashtanga (which is very demanding and requires doing a series of poses over and over again until perfected), or restorative (gentle practice that centers your breath and relaxation). Some like to take classes with one or two specific teachers. And that's great. In the beginning, especially, it's important to explore what works for your body, to see what studios feel the most comfortable and which teachers address injuries or help newcomers best.

These days yoga is a lifestyle for me—not because it keeps me in shape or is a cool trend but because it literally saved me. Not only was one debilitating skeletal issue completely healed in my lower back, but other nagging issues (that most of us just write off as an "old sports injury" or "something that happens when you get older") dramatically improved.

I'd had a recurring and incredibly painful dislocated shoulder (it pops out and won't go back until someone jams it back in), along with another separated shoulder (it pops out but goes back in—still painful, but only for a few seconds). Suffice it to say that I had very limited range of motion in both shoulders. I wouldn't even dream of reaching back to grab my driver's-side seat belt with my left hand, preferring to risk death rather than have another stab of pain. With yoga, this range of motion began to return. I have never regained complete mobility, but what I did get back felt like a miracle.

In addition, I had never been able to squat without being extremely uncomfortable. My knees were tight and really noisy when I got down low, like a machine that hadn't been properly oiled for years. This changed as well, and I soon was able to squat with ease. Just doing child's pose helped loosen up my knees so I could squat, and most everything I did in yoga helped loosen up my shoulders. It's really amazing how yoga opens you up physically and spiritually over time.

Perhaps more important, yoga changed my perspective. Even in the madness of startup hours and crowded airports, I could feel myself slow down and breathe. I was used to going fast—on the basketball court, lifting heavier and heavier weights at the gym, climbing the financial and then entrepreneurial ladders. But that pace no longer appealed to me. I began to see that I needed to practice "easy" instead of "hard." I realized that when you force things—a career, a relationship—life will be forceful back. If you want your life to be easy, you need to practice easy. Yoga isn't about pushing yourself into poses or competing with the person next to you. Yoga is about making yourself a better listener: to your mind, to your body, and to the world around you. This is something that Tara and Michael really ingrained in me at Strala.

With time, I began to make radical changes in my life. First of all, my diet changed. For a guy who used to hate vegetables, I was eating a lot more greens. My group of friends began to change as well. I started to become more aware of people's energy and how it was either draining or inspiring. I immersed myself in the yoga community, where I made lifelong friendships with the people with whom I studied.

Eventually yoga became a practice that my wife, Colleen, and I shared. We often went to class together, and that brought us closer. We sometimes walked into a class with tension between us and walked out holding hands, ready to talk. I became more in tune with my body. When something wasn't feeling right or when I felt stressed, rather than run away from it, I ran toward it. I asked myself questions like, "What's going on in my life?" "Where is there resistance?" "Where is there ease?" "What do I want more of, and what do I want less of?"

Of course there are other ways to move. If yoga isn't for you, the options include swimming, going for long walks, bike riding, jogging, taking dance classes—any form of movement that you enjoy and will stick with. What moves you?

You can be unbelievably fit in a physical sense,
but if you are not connected spiritually you lack a
wholeness that undermines your actuality and
potential as a complete person.

—RICH ROLL

When I experienced debilitating back pain in my midthirties, at first I assumed it was caused by mechanical issues in my lower back. Was it my old basketball injury combined with frequent flying that could be causing such a disruption in my body? It still didn't dawn on me that my mind was connected to my body, that in fact they are one, or that my mind was more powerful than I could imagine. I didn't even think about the fact that at the time I was very worried about money. I was concerned about paying bills as well as paying for our business, not to mention affording an engagement ring for the love of my life, Colleen.

I didn't make this connection until I sat on a massage table in San Francisco. I was at one of my favorite spas, International Orange, or IO for short. After hearing about my lower back pain, a therapist suggested I read a book called *Chakras and Their Archetypes*. Afterward I hobbled as fast as I could up Fillmore Street to our apartment and ordered the book. I'll never forget reading the section about the root chakra, an area of the lower back. It said that the root chakra often flares up because of *money worries*. I wasn't much of a New Age guy at the time, but I became one that day. The more I read, the more I learned not only about the New Age perspective on stress and the power of the mind to heal but also about the science that was catching up with it. My journey was just beginning.

Believe That You Can Heal

THIS BACK CRISIS WAS AT a very early stage in my wellness journey. I didn't have access to all the experts and doctors who are well versed in healing that I do now. Nor did I spend a lot of time on the Internet, Googling "L-4-L-5, S-1" or "sciatica" to read about all the awful stories of people who are living in pain.

I just thought I'd explore this yoga thing that I'd heard about. Hopefully it would work, and I'd avoid surgery. And if it didn't work, then I'd have to have surgery, and I'd be okay. The key was that I believed 100 percent that I'd be all right. I didn't believe for one minute that I wouldn't be able to walk.

I've since learned that my belief that "whatever happens, I'll be okay" might have been the real secret to my healing.

When we are no longer able to change a situation,
we are challenged to change ourselves.

—VIKTOR FRANKL, *MAN'S SEARCH FOR MEANING*

Fast-forward to late 2012, when we received the following e-mail to our general inbox at mindbodygreen:

Hi there,

I'm an Australian producer of a new documentary called The Connection. *It's a film about how modern science is catching up with ancient wisdom and proving that there really is a connection between our mind and body. The film will be featuring experts in the science and medical field, but we are currently searching for compelling case studies to support the interviews. Naturally, our research has led us to Jason and his story. I'm hoping that I may be able to get in touch to explore the possibility of him appearing in our film. We will be heading to the States for our interviews in the first two weeks of Feb.*

Hope someone can help put me in touch.

Kind regards,
Shannon Harvey

First I thought, "Is this for real? Someone actually wants to put me in a film?" Then I realized that if they had the science to support this concept of the mind-body connection, it must be really powerful stuff. Shannon and her film crew came to New York for a few months, and they interviewed me about my healing journey. In the process I discovered even more about how to heal my back.

It has now been almost three years since I first met Shannon and her crew. Her film, *The Connection,* premiered at the Clay Theatre on Fillmore Street in San Francisco. I even led a discussion after the screening. I shared the billing with all the expert doctors in the film, such as Dr. Andrew Weil, Dr. Herbert Benson, and Dr. Dean Ornish, and with some people like me who had healed themselves.

Colleen and I admired the film, and we spoke about the coincidence that the theater where the San Francisco premiere took place was right across the street from our old apartment, where my back first fell to pieces. Just seven years before, I had been hobbling around, barely able to walk. This was the first time we'd returned to San Francisco since we moved to New York. And oddly enough, here we were where it all began.

For me, yoga (and the belief that I could heal) were the keys to stress management and recovery from back pain. For you, it might be power walking, jogging, or hitting the gym. Anything that gets you away from your desk and moving around is a key aspect of well-being. Stick with it, but don't be rigid about it.

—— Grow Your Life Savings: Move ——

MY YOGA TEACHER FRIENDS ALL say that one of the most common reasons people come to yoga is for attunement with their bodies and their lives. Stress relief is the most frequent motivator. I asked my good friend, rock star yoga instructor Kathryn Budig, to share her four favorite stress-beating yoga poses.

FOUR YOGA POSES THAT RELIEVE
STRESS EVERY TIME

1. **Legs Up the Wall.** This is my favorite go-to pose. It reverses blood flow, relieves leg strain, and makes you slow down. Simply lie on the ground with your hips against the floorboard and bring one leg at a time up onto the wall. You can also place a pillow or bolster under your hips for a slight elevation and relief for the spine. Stay here for five to ten minutes, cover your eyes with an eye pillow or cloth, and let the pose do the work.

2. **Seated Meditation.** Sit on the floor, or prop yourself up on a pillow, if that is more comfortable. Inhale deeply, and on exhale chant "om" or another mantra or word you find soothing. Do so for at least two minutes. Continue to sit, focusing on breathing in and out through the nose with your eyes closed or with a soft gaze at the ground. If chanting feels too unfamiliar or woo-woo, simply inhale deeply while imagining good energy coming in, and exhale fully visualizing negative energy going out.

3. **Supine Twist.** We hold so much stress in the spine, but we often need just a simple twist to release blocked energy. This one is relaxing, reclined, and always delicious. Lie on your back with your knees tucked into your chest. Let them both drop to the side, keeping your knees stacked. Allow the opposite shoulder to melt to the ground as you lengthen your tailbone. Take eight breaths, and then switch sides.

4. **Standing Forward Fold.** Bend forward from your waist, keeping your knees bent slightly, feet pressing into the ground. Hold

on to your forearms and sway gently side to side, letting them hang, and relaxing your neck. This is a great way to release the body and let go of annoying, stressful thoughts. If this bothers your lower back, bend your knees further. If you have the flexibility, you can straighten your legs, keeping your hips stacked over your heels. For further relaxation, you can lean your hips against a wall, allowing it to keep you balanced and rooted.

A QUICK DEPOSIT IN YOUR WELLTH ACCOUNT

- In terms of overall health, moving every day is a must. If you're a couch potato, start with a fifteen-minute daily walk and add time and speed from there.
- Yoga is a great way to improve flexibility, ease pain, and deal with stress. It can be life-changing.
- There are several different types of yoga, so experiment and see which works best for you.
- Whatever you decide in terms of working out, make sure you really enjoy it so you stick with it. But don't be rigid about it. As Tim Ferriss said in his great book *The 4-Hour Body*, "The decent method you follow is better than the perfect method you quit." So find something that you will follow!

CHAPTER 3

Work

WHAT WE DO FOR WORK is not only about creating material wealth. Earning our daily bread should be fulfilling and rewarding, not just a job to pay the bills. But how do we muster the energy—or time or resources—to shake things up if we aren't satisfied in our careers? How do we make radical changes if we're too afraid or exhausted to do so? How do we transform what we do for money into true wellth? In this chapter, we will explore these questions. I hope the following story illustrates why it's so important to add passion to what you do for a living.

Success without fulfillment is the ultimate failure.

—TONY ROBBINS, *UNLEASH THE POWER WITHIN*

It was Christmas Eve 2014, and once again my mother had turned the house I grew up in into a winter wonderland. It had been more work for her because my grandmother had recently passed away. Together they could pull off a Christmas dinner for fifteen, but one person doing it all was tough. Even so, Mom still managed it.

My cousins, my great-aunt—who was my beloved grandmother's sister—and my aunt and uncle were there, all fifteen of us. My uncle is my mother's only sibling, and he is my only uncle. He is also my godfather. He spent a lot of time in our house when I was growing up, playing catch and taking me to museums. In many ways, he was a father to me when my own dad wasn't around.

My uncle Fred is really sharp, and he's a big guy, a burly six foot four. I always joke that height is everywhere in my family—even our dogs then were huge! Uncle Fred got his MBA and became a commercial real estate lender after he graduated. He traveled all around the world and always brought me back a T-shirt. Funny how as a kid, something like that means so much to you. In his late twenties, together with a few partners, he bought a deli in the garment district of Manhattan. It did so well that they bought a second deli. My mother did the books, and every once in a while I'd get to come with her. I loved going there because I could eat whatever I wanted—especially those big Toblerone chocolate bars.

Uncle Fred met his wife while working at the counter one day. Within a few years he had his first child, a boy, and a girl followed a year later. Around this time he decided that he wanted more stability for his growing family, so he went back to the banking business.

No matter what Uncle Fred does, he really works hard. And he always puts others first. He did this for the next thirty years. He'd leave for work at seven a.m. and often wouldn't get home until nine p.m. He'd wear worn-down shoes, not because he couldn't afford new ones but because he didn't feel good about spending on himself when he could buy things for his family instead. He never took real vacations, either. Vacations were usually just spent at home, resting. But he wasn't even good at that, as he'd often drive around looking at properties that were loan prospects. The older he got, the more worried he became that he'd be laid off because of his age. He never got laid off, and finally, just before his seventieth birthday, he decided to retire.

So on Christmas Eve of that year, Uncle Fred was finally free from the workforce. Finally free to take a vacation. Finally free to spend money on himself and not just everyone else. Finally free to enjoy life and get back to traveling, to visit places like Alaska, which we just discovered was somewhere he'd always wanted to go. That night, however, the once-burly man was now barely 180 pounds. He wobbled as he slowly went up the stairs. The guy who used to look like he could belly up to any bar and have a beer and a laugh with you was tired and gaunt from chemotherapy—so much so that he had to go to my old childhood bedroom and take a nap.

You see, just after he retired, he was diagnosed with colon cancer. He didn't even have a full month to enjoy retirement before he was diagnosed. He worked nonstop for almost fifty years to finally get to that retirement finish line, bypassing vacations, bypassing self-care (I don't think he even knows what self-care is!), bypassing anything that brought him joy, in order to save some extra money and provide for his family. But we can't be there for our families if we don't learn how to care for ourselves.

As I type these words, a year has passed, and now my uncle

is cancer-free. He's eating the cleanest diet he's ever eaten—we've got him juicing and eating lots of greens, and he's off sugar, especially the soda he was addicted to. Now he's talking about going to Bermuda and doing some traveling. He has a second chance to start enjoying his life and not just working to get to the finish line—a finish line in a race that, it turned out, wasn't worth winning.

You are the master of your destiny. You can influence, direct and control your own environment. You can make your life what you want it to be.

—NAPOLEON HILL, *THINK AND GROW RICH*

Make Sure You're Climbing the Right Ladder

MANY PEOPLE HAVE THEIR OWN uncle Freds. In fact, a lot of us *are* Uncle Fred and get caught up trying to win the wrong race. Until recently I was there, too.

A few years ago, as I told you earlier, I was constantly flying all over the country for work. I flew so often that I obtained status with the airline, which meant I got upgraded to business class. At six foot seven, to me that was the best thing ever, because I could barely fit into an economy seat.

The first time I got upgraded, I was hooked. But of course, there are levels of status. United Airlines, my airline of choice at the time, offered premier status at 25,000 miles flown; premier executive at 50,000; and then something called 1K at 100,000 miles. When you joined the 1K club at United, a whole new world seemed to open up. You'd hear rumors like "If you're 1K, you'll get upgraded on 95 percent of your flights. They'll literally bump someone from a flight to get you a seat if you need it."

That year I reached premier status pretty quickly, and it became apparent that I was going to have a shot at the 1K club if I flew consistently with United. I was excited about reaching such a milestone, and at times I'd even pay a bit more to fly with them. I was on a mission to get to 1K and enter this whole new world where my six-foot-seven body would reap the benefits of frequent flying!

Then I got to 50,000. I was still excited about getting to that 100,000-miles milestone, but I wasn't as enthusiastic as I had been in the beginning. I felt like I was in the scene in the film *Swingers*. Jon Favreau and Vince Vaughn are driving from L.A. to Vegas and shouting at the top of their lungs, "Vegas, baby, Vegas!" as they leave. Then about two hours into their long road trip, you can barely hear them moan the words, "Vegas, baby, Vegas." I was starting to feel the same way. Flying constantly was becoming tiresome. It was also making my bad back a lot worse. Sure, I had more comfortable seats with a lot more space to stretch my legs, but I was still in an airline seat.

At one point I saw the legendary pro golfer Gary Player being interviewed by Charlie Rose. One of the fittest and healthiest players on the PGA Tour, Gary was talking about being vegetarian, as well as his workout regime. He went on to say that the one thing that really aged him was all the flying he'd done over the years. That statement hit home.

When I got to around 85,000 miles, I was in the homestretch, so close to landing that coveted 1K status. I was on my laptop reviewing all the remaining business trips I had to make that year. In an effort to reach 1K, I started looking to see if I could take connections rather than fly direct. As I was starting to map out a plan, I paused for a moment and winced in pain as my lower back acted up.

Suddenly I had a moment of clarity. I thought, "Wait, why do I even *want* to fly 100,000 miles? This is exhausting. It's wearing me down. My back pain is getting worse. All this time I've been working toward this goal. But now that I'm almost there, I realize it's not worth achieving—it's affected my health and happiness. On top of that, I must be losing my mind by booking connecting flights just to get the miles, when direct flights are available!"

I didn't make 1K that year. And although I still have to fly a lot for work, I hope now that I never reach that milestone.

I'm just talking about a year that I spent flying. But what a metaphor for life and the career choices we make! What if I pursued a career path that involved spending eighty-plus hours a week slaving away, climbing the corporate ladder to success, getting promotion after promotion, and twenty years later getting all the way to the proverbial top? What if after all that, I realized that I had got on the wrong ladder? What if I spent my entire life pursuing a goal that wasn't fulfilling, that wasn't right for me—that was just plain wrong?

*Our job in this life is not to shape ourselves into some ideal
we imagine we ought to be, but to find out who we already
are and become it.*

—STEVEN PRESSFIELD, *THE WAR OF ART*

People often find themselves climbing the wrong ladder, and honestly, I don't know if there's an easy way out. Getting off that proverbial ladder or deciding not to run that race—especially when you've already achieved some success—is difficult. How do you know when you need to step off the treadmill? Physical stress (such as my back acting up) is one way to tell that work pressure is getting to you.

Our stress follows us everywhere, but when it becomes too much, its nature changes. It manifests itself in different ways and tends to hit you where you're most vulnerable. Stress can manifest itself externally, especially in a weakened part of your body. After I dislocated my left shoulder, it would twitch whenever I was stressed. A parasite rocked my gut (and microbiome), and my stomach would become extra sensitive after I was stressed from travel or lack of sleep. Stress will always be in your life, so you have to figure out how to deal with it. But when stress seems relentless and is always associated with work, it may be time to consider stepping off the hamster wheel.

Signs that you're overwhelmed with work pressure can include difficulty falling asleep, dreading going into the office every day, daydreaming while at work, or being depressed. You may begin to resent your boss or coworkers when they've done nothing to deserve it. You may fantasize about other people's jobs or situations, or about a time before you had so many responsibilities. But the key sign that you probably need to make a major change is simply that you're unhappy much of the time.

If this is the case, it's time to reexamine your career choices. You may even have to start over and move into an entirely different career or field. But before you decide it's time for a do-over, you have to go deep and ask yourself some hard questions. How do you know when it's time to ask these questions? I think it's actually pretty black and white. If you're even remotely thinking that you might be working where you're not really supposed to be, then you should be asking these questions. If not, this idea won't pull at you that much.

Spending time in the business and self-help sections of the bookstore helped me tremendously—especially books like *What Color Is Your Parachute*, *The Artist's Way*, *Flow*, and *Unlimited Power*. But do be sure that you aren't going in the "grass is always greener" direction. If you're basically satisfied in your career with the normal ups and downs—as opposed to feeling miserable at the very thought of going into the office—then you're probably fine where you are.

What is it that I really want out of life?

What makes me happy? What doesn't make me happy?

What does career satisfaction look like to me?

How can I live this way and still support myself and possibly my family?

Stopping to ask these questions and then actually taking action doesn't guarantee that the right door will open immediately; it can take years. It took me *seven* years. But I will guarantee that if you truly listen to yourself and do the work required to figure out a desired career path, the right door will appear—and you'll run through it and accomplish your goals with more passion and success than you ever imagined.

When one door of happiness closes, another opens; but often we look so long at the closed door that we do not see the one which has been opened for us.

—HELEN KELLER, *TO LOVE THIS LIFE*

We're Good at Going Fast but Need to Go Slow

WE TYPE A'S ARE THE world's best at going fast. We get more done in a day than some do in a week. We've become so good at running (and catching) that subway. Getting in that extra meeting. Even stacking our social calendars so we can run from our weekend fitness class straight to our coffee date, then to our lunch date, then to God knows what. And that's on a day off. We are so freaking good at getting stuff done. Not only do we get it all done, we get it done fast. We kick ass and take names. We work hard and play hard. We are our own masters of the universe, living life to the fullest. Or not.

I believe this attitude is all wrong. Every person who is

succeeding by means of brute force and speed isn't doing it correctly. Sure, we can get things done this way, but we're making life a lot more difficult than it needs to be. We're also being a lot harder on our minds and bodies. This isn't some New Age cliché; we truly do need to get better at slowing down.

If we can learn to slow down, we end up accomplishing more and doing so with less effort. There are two practices that help me slow down: yoga and meditation. You can also go for a long walk, get exercise, keep a journal, listen to soothing music, take a nap, do stretches, reread your favorite books, or relax in nature. What works for me isn't necessarily what works for you.

Be like water making its way through cracks. Do not be assertive, but adjust to the object, and you shall find a way around or through it. If nothing within you stays rigid, outward things will disclose themselves.
Empty your mind, be formless. Shapeless, like water.
If you put water into a cup, it becomes the cup. You put water into a bottle and it becomes the bottle. You put it in a teapot, it becomes the teapot. Now, water can flow or it can crash. Be water, my friend.

—BRUCE LEE, *TAO OF JEET KUNE DO*

Think about all the amazing things that have happened in your life: whether it was meeting your partner or spouse or landing your dream job. How fast and hard did you push for either? Odds are, it just happened. I'm sure you put in the work and laid the foundation, whether it was by having your heart broken in previous relationships so you grew and were ready for your soul mate, or putting in all those extra hours at the office so you rose faster than anyone at the company.

Whenever I feel like I'm stuck at work—when I'm not making the type of progress I want or I'm faced with some sort of mental block—I find that the breakthrough comes from a balance of pushing through and letting go. I'll push and push, and then at a certain point, I let go. It's taken me years to find the perfect balance of when to go for a walk, to meditate, or go to the gym—or just do something where I can get out of my head. I also mindfully set an intention when I get to this point. I will say to myself that I'm open and willing to accept the right next steps, whatever they may be.

In his great book *10% Happier,* Dan Harris tells a story about David Axelrod. At the time, Axelrod was running President Obama's reelection campaign when so many terrible global factors—such as the European debt crisis, al-Qaeda, Israel, and Iran—were out of the administration's control. When Axelrod was pressed about all these seemingly never-ending challenges, he responded, "All we can do is everything we can do." To that response, I'd add: *And then we need to let go.*

When my first three employees and I were moving into our brand-new office at mindbodygreen, I wanted everything to be perfect. I'd hoped that everyone would feel like they were a part of something special on that first day, so I had business cards, notebooks, pens, brand-new iMacs, and ergonomic chairs ready to go. But the desks I had ordered turned out to be terrible, and I had less than forty-eight hours to get replacements. I started to freak out, as I thought this would leave a horrible impression on our new team members. After all, they had left the corporate world behind (and taken a pay cut) to risk working at a startup—a startup with no desks!

After panicking for a few minutes, I decided to take action. I figured one place in New York City that had lots of random furniture was the Bowery, where there were lots of restaurant suppliers. I took a moment and decided to let go of the situation and believe that everything would be okay no matter what happened. Then I went to the Bowery, where I found our desk supplier within five minutes. His desks were higher quality and less expensive than what we had previously, and we've been buying our desks from him ever since.

Happy is harder than money. Anybody who thinks money will make you happy hasn't got money.

—DAVID GEFFEN, PRODUCER AND FILM STUDIO EXECUTIVE

My point isn't that you should slack off, but that you need to choose the things that matter and not go full on at every single thing. This is the type A challenge that many of us struggle with, myself included. We can just work harder and faster, trying to break down a door that's not ready to open. We can also work *smarter* and be ready for a different door that will open easily. It's finding the balance that's so hard. Prioritize but don't obsess.

Working Hard Gets You Only So Far

JUST BECAUSE YOU'RE WORKING SIXTEEN hours a day doesn't mean you're being efficient with your time. Most of us—aside from those extraordinarily lucky few—have to work hard to succeed. But if you're not also organized and efficient, you're just wasting time.

In a lot of corporate cultures or social circles, it's almost a badge of honor to work until two a.m. or pull an all-nighter. And in some jobs when you're on tight deadlines, working all hours is a necessary evil. But often it's not. Not really. When I'm focusing on things that I'm good at, I tend to produce good work, and I do so very quickly. When I work on things that I'm not good at, I tend to work much slower and produce results that are just okay. At times you have to focus on stuff that doesn't play to your strengths, but whenever possible, try to delegate that type of assignment to someone else on your team who is better suited to it.

If you're a manager with employees who work for you, or if you're an entrepreneur, learning to delegate is key. Initially, you probably will do everything yourself. But as your responsibilities or your business grows, and you bring on additional hires, you have to let go of trying to do everything yourself—especially of the stuff that you're not great at. Otherwise you'll find yourself working even harder and longer than ever before.

So how do you know if you're working smart or just working too hard? For me, it's about playing to my strengths and finding my flow.

It is when we act freely, for the sake of the action itself rather than for ulterior motives, that we learn to become more than what we were. When we choose a goal and invest ourselves in it to the limits of concentration, whatever we do will be enjoyable. And once we have tasted this joy, we will redouble our efforts to taste it again. This is the way the self grows.

—MIHALY CSIKSZENTMIHALYI, *FLOW: THE PSYCHOLOGY OF OPTIMAL EXPERIENCE*

How do we find our flow? Here's an example. One night you're up until two a.m. trying to finesse a financial model that doesn't seem to add up the way you want it to. This is a task that maybe the accountant or a math whiz coworker should be doing. It's another thing altogether to be up until two a.m. writing about a topic that excites you. In that case the words stream out, and before you know it, six hours have gone by. Yes, you've still worked a pretty long day, but there's a difference. You've found your flow, that state where time almost stops, and you're totally caught up in what you're doing. Developers tend to find themselves in a state of flow when they're coding, as do artists when they're painting, musicians when they're composing, and anyone who loves what they do when they're doing it.

Everywhere we look in business, timetables once measured by calendars can now be clocked by egg timers. So how can we keep up? In a word—and according to an

*ever-increasing pile of evidence—"flow." Technically defined
as an "optimal state of consciousness where we feel our
best and perform our best," the term takes its name from
the sensation it confers. In flow, every action,
every decision, arises seamlessly from the last. In this
state, we are so focused on the task at hand that all
else falls away. Action and awareness merge.
Our sense of self vanishes. Our sense of time distorts.
And performance goes through the roof.*

**—STEVEN KOTLER, JOURNALIST AND COFOUNDER OF
THE FLOW GENOME PROJECT**

When you find your flow, you're not really working. You're not forcing yourself to work; instead, you're lost in creation and concentration. Find your flow, and you'll produce the greatest, most fulfilling work of your entire life. Are you in flow—able to focus intently on what you're doing, rather than checking your watch every five minutes? Or are you wasting time? Time is our greatest resource—savor it.

Think Ahead Three Moves

IF YOU'RE LOOKING FOR YOUR dream job or simply want to change careers, you should also think three moves ahead. Advance yourself incrementally, while keeping in mind where you want to wind up ultimately. My wife, Colleen, is a perfect example of using strategic career moves to get where she wanted to be.

Colleen's background was in fashion and retail; she spent seven years at Old Navy/Banana Republic. But like me, Colleen was passionate about wellness and wanted to get out of the fashion box. Her next job was as a senior buyer at Walmart. Now, anyone who looked at Colleen's résumé didn't see her as someone who worked exclusively in fashion. Colleen's next move was to Amazon, where she ran women's apparel for its fashion flash sale site. Even though the position was in fashion, it was in e-commerce, and at the largest e-commerce player in the world. She was out of the proverbial fashion box. So when an up-and-coming juice company in New York was looking for someone who could help with merchandising, buying, and e-commerce, someone who knew how to build systems that could scale and be operationally efficient, Colleen's experience at Walmart and Amazon got her the job that eventually brought her to wellness.

Colleen was thrilled to be working in the wellness field, but the job was a disaster. Finding a position in your passion isn't necessarily a panacea. But it still brought her one step closer to her dream position. Those jobs were three moves ahead, but her last and best move would be to mindbodygreen. Nepotism? Perhaps, although I demanded more of Colleen than of anyone we'd ever hired. For starters, in the early days of mbg, she pitched in by working nights and weekends (she did this for three years). Then she came on full-time as an unpaid intern for two months to prove to the team that she could actually sell and grow revenue, which was her job. Then she took a massive pay cut. She still works harder than just about anyone else in the company.

Thinking ahead three moves is a great way to approach not

only the job market but life. Strategize about how to gain a particular skill set, embrace a practice, or take a specific job that will bring you closer to your ultimate goal. One of the easiest and most actionable things you can do is free: use LinkedIn. Go find people who have the dream job you want, and check out how they got there. Some paths are fairly linear, with people specializing early on in their career, while other paths are curvier and more interesting, with people on them from diverse backgrounds.

Identify as many of these people as possible, and then see how you're connected to them. Try to get an introduction through a mutual connection. You'd be surprised how easy this is and how approachable people are, especially when they're connected through a mutual acquaintance. Malcolm Gladwell talks about the power of "weak links" in *The Tipping Point;* many professional websites like LinkedIn are a wealth of weak links that can help get you started! It probably won't be one of your five closest friends who ends up helping you land your next job. Instead, your friends of friends who have their own network of friends—your weak links—will wind up being your strongest connectors when you're job hunting. And when you're perusing a site such as LinkedIn, I'll bet you become inspired by the diversity of paths and backgrounds as you begin thinking three moves ahead. Think three moves ahead, realizing that it may not be the first or second job that leads you to the ideal position.

Fitting Your Career with Your Passion

I HAD ALWAYS ENJOYED READING about entrepreneurs like Oprah, Richard Branson, and Steve Jobs, people who were not only incredibly successful but also loved their work so much that they were incredibly excited about every aspect of it. People who felt that their careers reflected their personalities. I knew that I wanted this type of life. I wanted to build a company that I was passionate about—a company that inspired people to live better. I also loved media and creative freedom. I wanted to be a part of something that represented who I was as a person.

When I first decided I wanted to become an entrepreneur in 2002, I had no idea how it would take shape. I started, or was part of, companies that had some of these qualities. I looked at each as an opportunity to learn and to help me create that larger, more ambitious vision. It took me ten years to find it, but I never would have found it if I'd been stuck on discovering my dream business or dream job from day one.

It's so easy to be fixated on a certain title at a certain company, or to become obsessed with a certain product or company that we want to launch. But this is far too narrow. First, what if the title is all wrong for you, or the product is all wrong for the market? Second, what's your motivation for doing what you're doing in the first place? Odds are, if you're looking to start a business, then you want to solve a problem for people, and at the same time you desire creative or financial freedom. If you're looking for a specific title within a company, you probably crave the responsibility and potential for growth that comes along with that title. If it's just the status and title alone that you want, then you're in it for the wrong reasons.

Only those who risk going too far can possibly find out how far they can go.

—T. S. ELIOT, PREFACE TO *TRANSIT OF VENUS*

Before you even think about starting a new business or going for a big promotion, focus on *why* you want what you want. Reflect upon the qualities that this business or position possesses. Hone in on what you want to learn, who you want to meet, and what you want to build. But definitely don't get hung up on having your dream scenario presented to you on a silver platter. If you do, you'll probably be waiting a lifetime for something that may never come. Yet as I mentioned, learning to think three moves ahead can make the wait much shorter.

Thinking three moves ahead means that you should focus on what you want out of your career, and how you're going to create value through your work (along with how you're going to make money). But be prepared to pivot at any movement. Don't get stuck trying to jam a square peg into a round hole.

Some of the most successful careers and businesses came as the result of pivoting. Did you know that Instagram began as Burbn, a check-in app that had a gaming element? It didn't perform well, so the founders regrouped and got rid of all the features except photo sharing. Then they relaunched it as

Instagram, and the rest is history. This is a great example of why it's not good to get stuck on a particular idea.

Your time is limited, so don't waste it living someone else's life.

—STEVE JOBS, STANFORD COMMENCEMENT ADDRESS, JUNE 12, 2005

Grow Your Life Savings: Work

MY GOOD FRIEND SCOTT MACKINLAY HAHN, cofounder and CEO of Loomstate, has this advice to offer about finding a dream job:

When we talk about "job satisfaction" or "career evaluation," there are usually two camps. If you are privileged or perhaps empowered to be in the smaller group of folks who have more options and opportunity, ironically you may also have a tougher time being ultimately "gratified" than the majority of us, who have weightier responsibilities and commitments that may limit how we go about a career-change evaluation.

To be clear, the mindset of seeking career joy is fundamental and essential, regardless of our means of landing the "dream job." Turning work into play and essentially serving others, while reducing suffering (for others), is the highest compensation one can seek. Everyone has unique attributes and desires that make their journey special. My own guiding principle is to strive for a balance between self-expression and self-sacrifice. Ultimately, we are happiest and most fulfilled when we are constantly developing (learning), part of a thriving resilient community, and uniquely acknowledged for our individual contributions.

It's always healthy to stop and reflect on your career satisfaction, and to adjust course where necessary. If you are truthful with yourself and live in an examined way, the signs will be everywhere—either indicating whether change is necessary or affirming that you are right where you need to be. A practical approach is to evaluate some fundamentals: a series of if/then questions to arrive at critical decision points that guide action. Engage your "career GPS" to know where you stand. Start with more extreme questions and work toward the nuances of your desires. Try asking ones like those that follow:

What are you good at? Where do you see yourself in five to ten years' time? What type of lifestyle makes you happiest? Where do you want to be working and what type of people do you want to surround yourself with? Are you working for a robber baron capitalist, and/or do you dread going to work every day?

Do you share the values of the company you work for or the clients you serve? How did you arrive in your current role? (Were you recruited, or did you seek the position?) Do you have dependents and mouths to feed, significant debt, or student loans? (Perhaps these will limit one's options, but never compromise in terms of foundational principles and ethics.) Are you currently working in your preferred or trained field, or in "just a job" where you often imagine doing something else?

As you start to see where you fall, and how you answer, the fun can begin with fine-tuning career adjustments toward your satisfaction.

Balancing our satisfaction and fulfillment in work and our personal lives is an art and a science. By examining our fundamental needs and health requirements, we can prioritize our related choices and preferences. People who make the effort to figure out what they really want in their careers are usually happier in life because, having evaluated their work situations, they can take planned action to change them for the better.

A QUICK DEPOSIT IN YOUR WELLTH ACCOUNT

- Physical symptoms of stress can be signs that you need to leave the rat race and explore something else more meaningful to you career-wise.

- You have to work hard to succeed, but if you're not also organized and efficient, you're just wasting time.
- If you're an individual, try to advance incrementally in your career, always keeping in mind where you want to wind up. If you're an entrepreneur, focus on what you want out of the business, and how you're going to create value (along with how you're going to make money). In each case, be prepared to pivot at any movement.
- Being in flow, when you're using both knowledge and creativity to accomplish a task, is the most pleasing and productive form that work can take. You can tell you're there when you have no consciousness of the passage of time.

CHAPTER 4

Believe

BELIEF IN ONESELF IS A huge factor in successful careers, love, and life in general. In fact, it's one of the cornerstones of wellth. But how do we keep on believing when things don't seem to be going our way? What do we do when our attempts at school, work, or relationships are thwarted? How do we turn it around?

Visualization can be a big part of belief, and it has three elements: believing, seeing, and, doing. (I'll describe each of these components a little later on in this chapter.)

Believe you can, and you're halfway there.

—THEODORE ROOSEVELT

We also must believe that the universe has our back, and that we are at the place where we need to be, at the correct time in our lives. This attitude isn't being fatalistic or giving up; instead, it's accepting that the universe has a plan for us of which we may not yet be aware. And if you don't believe in God or a universal spirit, then perhaps a general sense of optimism can sustain you. If you're not much of a believer in optimism, a 2015 study at the University of Illinois concluded that "individuals with the highest levels of optimism have twice the odds of being in ideal cardiovascular health compared to their more pessimistic counterparts." So at the very least, optimism can make your heart stronger.

One way to continue to believe—even when the chips are down—is to realize that you can connect the dots only going backward.

You can't connect the dots going forward; you can only connect them looking backwards. So you have to trust that the dots will somehow connect in your future.

—STEVE JOBS, STANFORD COMMENCEMENT ADDRESS,
JUNE 12, 2005

Steve Jobs was right on the money with these words of wisdom from his now-famous commencement speech at Stanford. There have been so many times when, to my disappointment, a perceived opportunity didn't work out for me. Eventually, though, a much greater opportunity often came along. Only then was I able to see that the way things worked out was for the best, by far.

Connect the Dots Instance 1: I was in high school when I first saw *Animal House,* and I fell in love with that movie. Since it was based on a Dartmouth fraternity in the 1960s, I thought the college would be just like it was on the screen—one never-ending party, with kegs and togas and great boozy friendships.

I was the center for my high school basketball team, and my heart was set on playing at Dartmouth. And Dartmouth's head coach was all over me. He recruited me aggressively, driving down with his top assistant to woo my mother and me into committing to the school. The twist was that, at Ivy League schools, recruited athletes still had to apply and get accepted, whereas at non-Ivies, athletes just had to sign on the dotted line.

Rather than waiting until April and applying to all the Ivy League schools that were recruiting me, I decided to put all my eggs in one basket and commit to Dartmouth, since the coach said I was a shoo-in. But I wasn't. I didn't get in because my class rank was terrible. Class ranking, along with SAT and achievement scores, then made up the Academic Index, a formula that Ivy League schools used to determine whether recruited athletes were up to academic snuff.

At the time I was in shock, but now I'm glad I didn't get into Dartmouth. Coming from Long Island with its close proximity to New York City, I would've hated being in the middle of nowhere in New Hampshire, and I wouldn't have liked being at such a conservative school. I now know that I'd have been miserable there. Columbia was the perfect fit for me, and it was right in my backyard. If I hadn't gone to Columbia, I never would have met my wife, Colleen (we met through the sister of a mutual friend I went to college with); nor would I have made all the incredible friends I did or had the amazing experiences I had there. Of course, back then, not getting into Dartmouth seemed like a huge blow. Only in hindsight—connecting the dots backward—did it become clear that this was actually a great stroke of luck. Deciding between Dartmouth and Columbia was definitely a first-world problem, but to a seventeen-year-old kid, the world seemed to hang in the balance.

Hindsight is always 20-20.
—ANONYMOUS

Connect the Dots Instance 2: I had summer internships on Wall Street after my sophomore and junior years in college. I interned on the fixed-income trading floor at Prudential Securities. This was exactly where I wanted to be after reading the best-selling book *Liar's Poker* by Michael Lewis, which profiled the freewheeling days of bond trading at Salomon Brothers in the 1980s. I was enamored of the flamboyant lifestyle of the bond traders, not to mention the money they made. Bond traders seemed more sharp and sophisticated than everyone else on the Street, in every sense of the word—in the way they thought, the way they dressed, even the way they carried themselves with a bit of a swagger as they walked across the trading floor. At least it seemed that way to a twenty-two-year-old with little life experience.

Throughout my senior year at Columbia, I interviewed at all the big Wall Street firms for entry-level bond trading positions. In some instances, I didn't even make it past the first round because my grades were terrible. Naïvely, I had thought that since I was a college athlete who had worked my way through school, my poor grades wouldn't count against me. But I was wrong. I did manage to make it to the final round at Morgan Stanley, where I had a full day of interviews, one after the other, from eight a.m. to five p.m. All twelve interviews went great, with the exception of one woman who really homed in on my GPA. But I had a feeling that her vote counted the most, and in the end they didn't make me an offer.

Come graduation in May 1998, I still didn't have a job, although it wasn't due to a lack of effort. I kept on networking with Columbia alums, and I interviewed for any openings in bond trading. I was so excited to begin this next phase of my life that I bought five inexpensive suits with my graduation money. I figured I wouldn't have enough time to go shopping between the time I was hired and my start date. As it turned out, I wouldn't need those suits at all—but I'll come back to that.

I had thought Prudential would be my fallback since I had interned there and everyone liked me. I didn't really want to end up there because it wasn't as prestigious as the other firms. But I really needed a job, so I began talking to the head of the corporate bond trading desk, whom I knew from the previous summer. We had already discussed the trading assistant's salary—$28,000—but he said he had to wait on some formalities before he could offer me the job.

A trading assistant doesn't actually trade; instead, he or she shadows a trader, learning the ropes while doing clerical grunt work. Basically you're a glorified coffee boy. The position lasts for two years, and then if you're deemed good enough, you're allowed to begin trading. It wasn't my idea of a fabulous start, but I was desperate to begin working and earning. While I was living at home in the suburbs with my mom, my friends from college had already begun the next stages of their lives: living in Manhattan, earning money, going out to nice restaurants, and partying (which at the time to me was probably the most appealing aspect of being on my own).

I had saved $1,000, which wasn't much of a financial cushion. My friends were very generous and would pick up the tab whenever we'd go out. But I wanted to be independent; I didn't want to be a burden. I was also bored as hell. I'd try to keep busy by working out at the gym every day, which actually got me into the best shape of my life. I also spent hours at the local bookstore perusing finance books, but it wasn't enough. I was impatient for my new life to begin—but no matter how hard I pushed, it just wasn't happening.

Every week I'd check in with the head of the trading desk, but each time I was told, "Still waiting on the okay." Weeks went by. Then weeks became three months, and still no job offer. I had no idea that, behind the scenes, the bond market was being annihilated through the collapse of the monster bond hedge fund, Long-Term Capital Management. Eventually the government ended up bailing out LTCM with a $3.6 billion loan. At the same time, Prudential's entire floor of bond traders was being gutted. This was happening across Wall Street, as everyone was trying to cope with the aftermath of LTCM's demise and its cascading effect on the market. This meant that my dream career of becoming a bond trader wasn't going to happen.

By now it was September, and I'd been job-hunting for almost five months. I had already felt a sense of urgency, but now I was getting desperate. I'd interview for anything; I just wanted to work. I interviewed at a commercial real estate company, but the position had a delayed start date and I didn't want to wait. I even interviewed for a job selling photocopiers. The hiring manager glanced at my résumé, then looked at me and said, "You don't want this job. Trust me. You should work somewhere else."

Next I interviewed to be a stockbroker's assistant at a company where I'd have to make a hundred-plus cold calls per day, dialing for dollars. The HR guy was a former cheerleader for a college team, and he must have been treated badly by the players at his school because he acted like a real hard-ass. Most people who interview ex–college athletes don't question their work ethic, as it's kind of a prerequisite to be able to compete at that level. But this guy really tried to make a point about how hard his job was, and how hard *he* had worked as a cheerleader, and how the players sometimes dogged it. I couldn't get a word in. It felt less like a serious interview than like a therapy session, where I was the therapist as well as the punching bag. I didn't get that job, either.

During this time, three of my college buddies were trading equities at a proprietary day-trading firm called Heartland Securities. Basically the job was to trade the firm's money but with no interaction with clients. Working there, you were given carte blanche to go out and trade and make money. That was it. Your bonus was nonnegotiable; it was all in your P&L, or profit and loss statement. The more profit you generated for the firm, the more money you made. This was very appealing to someone who was hungry to start earning—me. My buddies were doing quite well, too—each was making over six figures in their second year.

I'd never considered applying to Heartland; my friends there took the positions only because they didn't have to wear suits, and they had complete autonomy. It was almost the anti–Wall Street firm in many ways, the opposite of the classic white-shoe, blueblood places, where it seemed as if everyone who worked there was a direct descendant from the *Mayflower*. This place was a complete meritocracy. It didn't matter who your parents were or what social clubs you belonged to, and there was no political jockeying at all. All they cared about was how smart you were, how competitive you were, and your ability to generate money. Suffice it to say, they loved Ivy League athletes.

Given my lack of prospects, I decided to interview at Heartland. The more I heard, the more I felt the job was for me. The starting salary was higher than at most Wall Street firms, and I loved the idea that within three months I'd be trading, whereas at other places I'd have to spend two years fetching coffee. Heartland hired me in November. I took the Series 7 & 63 exams required for my license to trade and started work on January 4, 1999. That year I made $70,000 ($40,000 in salary plus another $30,000 in commission). In 2000 I made over $800,000 ($40,000 salary and $760,000 in commission). And I never even had to wear a suit!

If I had gotten the job at Prudential, I would have been laid off one year later when the entire trading floor was dumped. If I had been hired by one of those prestigious bond trading firms, I never would have been as successful as I was in those first two years at Heartland. If I'd started as a trading assistant, it would have taken me at least five years to make that kind of money. The money was nice, but it isn't the point of the story. Most important, it would have taken me much longer to realize that money didn't buy me the type of happiness that I was looking for. It would have taken me much longer to find my purpose, new life path, and passion.

Thank God for all those unanswered prayers!

But as Steve Jobs said, you can't connect the dots going forward; you can only connect them going backward.

I have run into closed doors over and over in my life. I desperately want to go in one direction, yet no matter how hard I try to, I can't. It's as if I'm trying to bang open a door that's locked tight, but right next to it is the door I'm supposed to run effortlessly through. It has my name on it, but I just haven't realized it yet.

A very little key will open a very heavy door.
—CHARLES DICKENS, "HUNTED DOWN"

Connect the Dots Instance 3: After almost four years on Wall Street, I moved to Washington, D.C., to work on a health care startup. I got caught up in the political atmosphere and decided that I wanted to work on the Hill. I even interned for a congressman and applied for a job as a press secretary. But no one would hire me since my Wall Street experience was irrelevant, and I'd been an intern for only a few months. I would have given anything to land an entry-level job, so I could begin to build my new life in D.C. But I wasn't hired—and again, thank God for that! If I'd begun a career on the Hill, I'd probably still be living there, and mindbodygreen never would have happened.

Throughout my life, there have been many times when I've

worked so hard for something, or wanted something so badly, but the door was slammed in my face. If you've been living on this planet for any length of time, I'm sure the same has happened to you. Don't get me wrong, I believe in working hard and busting down doors, but at a certain point you have to let go and let God—or the universe—show you the way. It's almost as if you get to the point where you can't take it anymore and give up. You get on your knees and pray for guidance, and at that moment someone (or something) takes over.

Only then do you find what's best for you and not what you *think* is best for you. After that—although not always immediately thereafter—another door tends to open.

Sometimes good things fall apart, so better things can fall together.

—MARILYN MONROE

You can push yourself only so much, and then at some point you have to trust fate to show you the way. I believe that there are no accidents in life. Everything is connected, and where you are at this moment is precisely where you're supposed to be. You may not know why, and you may hate your current situation, but in time the reason will become clear.

When Terrible Things Happen

SOMETIMES IT WON'T BE EASY to accept drastic events, such as death, disease, or hardship. At times, really bad things happen to really good people. When they occur, there's no silver lining. There's no solace during our personal 9/11s. Sometimes we are never able to connect the dots in any direction.

When such events—such as the death of my father when I was in high school—happen to me, I have to put them in the "I don't know" drawer. I heard the renowned preacher Joel Osteen describe this concept on television, and it really resonated with me. When awful things occur, there are no answers to be found. Looking for the silver lining, looking to connect the dots, just leads to more pain. The only way to get out of this downward spiral is to let go of the search for answers. I realize that this is easy to say, but not easy to do. Deciding to put such events into the "I don't know" drawer is often the only thing that can help us move on from a tragedy.

I also believe that God/the universe/whatever-you-want-to-call-It tends to know your breaking point. This concept of "God knowing your breaking point" first came to me through an unlikely and somewhat polarizing source, Condoleezza Rice. In 2003 I heard Rice speak about her faith at a church in Washington, D.C. It was around the time that things were going badly in Iraq, and she was under fire. The press had been all over her, and she answered questions from the audience about how she relied on her faith to get through times like these. I was shocked that she'd be open to taking such questions from a town-hall-like meeting at a church, but she did.

After her speech, I realized that whenever I had felt that I couldn't take a situation anymore, something positive usually happened. One of my favorite quotes is by Henry Wadsworth Longfellow: "The lowest ebb is the turn of the tide." I have found this to be true in my life. I believe that God/the universe gives you only what you can handle and nothing beyond that. Sometimes that limit is more than you think possible. And the limit tends to grow with the more traumas you experience.

Courage is not something that you already have, that makes you brave when the tough times start. Courage is what you earn when you've been through the tough times and you discover they are not so tough, after all.

—MALCOLM GLADWELL, *DAVID AND GOLIATH*

Godwinks

SOMETIMES AN INTERVENTION OCCURS IN a small way— what inspirational author SQuire Rushnell calls "Godwinks." These Godwinks are little reminders that there's a light at the end of the tunnel, that someone is watching, and that you're on the right track.

At one point in my twenties, I was heartbroken after a breakup, the second one in a year. I was distraught, thinking, "Why would God do this to me again, after I just got out of a long and painful relationship? Why would He put me in another one, only to have it fall apart so horribly and suddenly?"

I felt empty and miserable, and no amount of fancy meals or giant bar tabs could ease the pain.

I was also still mourning the loss of my father, and yet I was moving too fast to even realize it, never mind process my loss. It depressed me that my success on Wall Street didn't bring me the happiness I had been sure it would. The one exception was the pleasure I got from giving away money and spending it on others. That was a lot more enjoyable than making it. I donated to causes that had meaning for me, like the basketball programs at Columbia University and Northfield Mount Hermon School, both of which had given me so much. I bought my mom a car. I bought dinners and drinks for all my friends. I spent so much money in one year at The Palm, a steakhouse near the theater district in Manhattan, that they put my face up on the wall. My caricature is sandwiched between those of Joe Namath and Adam Sandler—so I'm immortalized as "Who is that guy next to Namath and Sandler?" Spending on myself didn't fill my emptiness, but that in itself was an important lesson. Money becomes abundance only when you spread the wealth. For me at the time, this meant spreading a lot of martinis and steak. Good intentions, bad execution.

I was ripe for a wake-up call. For me, and for so many others, it was 9/11. It was after the attacks that I began to yearn for a sense of balance and contentment rather than the buzz and highs of my nightlife and my daily manic rush to the next dollar. I was surprised to find myself thinking about my purpose and significance, beyond my bank account. I also felt worn out. I was beginning to see that being healthy involved more than just looking good in the mirror. Since my job and my relationships at the time were fairly joyless, I wondered what would actually make me happy.

We all have had moments where we've asked, "Why me?" Don't get me wrong, my life was good at the time, my friends and family were healthy, and I was successful in my career. Yet I was still very unhappy. The day after the breakup that I mentioned, I was taking the elevator in my office building and received a flattering comment from a very attractive woman before she got out at the next floor. It was precisely what I needed to hear at that moment, the perfect Godwink. Immediately a mental shift occurred, and I knew I was going to be okay. I realized that God was watching, that he had a plan, and that he knew my breaking point.

I've endured situations that were far more serious than a heart-shattering breakup. At times I've been down on my knees crying, feeling as if I couldn't take it anymore, ready to give up. But I've come to expect that the tide will always turn, often signaled by a Godwink, and the change will occur just as I've reached my breaking point.

This is the point where we need to let go and trust that the universe or God will give us what we need, although not necessarily what we want. Sometimes we do get what we want, and sometimes we don't. But only after the trauma has passed can we finally connect the dots backward and find a reason and meaning for what has occurred.

How can you connect the dots backward in your own life? Consider how you'd answer these questions:

Think about an instance where things did not turn out the way you wanted or expected. Was it the end of the world?

Now try to list one or two good things that resulted from not getting what you wanted, even if the benefit occurred several years later.

Name two other instances where connecting the dots backward reveals the silver lining in a perceived negative event.

Silver Linings

This is what I believe to be true . . . You have to do everything you can. You have to work your hardest. If you stay positive, you have a shot at a silver lining.

—PAT SOLATANO IN *SILVER LININGS PLAYBOOK*

I FIND THIS QUOTE FROM the film *Silver Linings Playbook* so powerful. It exemplifies the balance between staying positive and expecting good things to happen, while at the same time not being passive about it.

You can't just sit back and expect good things to happen. It requires hard work. One of my first big and painful silver linings was the third-degree sprain in my right foot that occurred during a basketball scrimmage. A third-degree sprain is worse than breaking a bone. Suffice it to say, the injury was ridiculously painful, and it was also very ill timed, as it hampered my speed and jumping ability and ultimately hurt my basketball career. I never recovered my former physical agility, and it took years to recover mentally. I had really been coming into my own as a player, drawing attention from Big East and Atlantic Coast Conference colleges. This led me to spend weeks upon weeks rehabbing. I felt pressured to come back as soon as possible, and thus I ended up damaging my right ankle permanently.

Yet this injury eventually changed my life for the better, because it helped me gain perspective. I still worked hard at rehabbing my ankle to get back to participating in games, but rather than being obsessed about playing basketball at a big-time Division 1 college, I started to think about playing at a school that was known more for its academics. I also began to see that injuries happened all the time, and not only to athletes. One day you could be healthy; the next, you could be in rehab fighting to get your body back to half of what it was capable of doing before. I had to think about what was really important to me, and I realized that life was a lot more than playing basketball.

This sprain was a silver lining that would forever change my thinking and my goals. In hindsight, I wouldn't have avoided the injury for anything in the world. My life has been filled with silver linings: breakups with girlfriends I was in love with but who would have driven me insane; seemingly ill-timed bathroom breaks that ultimately saved me from major financial losses as a trader; and potential investors who I thought were perfect but for no apparent reason didn't come through. In each instance, I was saved from major headaches and heartaches. I believe that our lives are filled with silver linings—but as Pat Solatano says, we just have to work hard for them.

You've Got to See It to Believe It

LUCKY PEOPLE HAVE THE ABILITY to see the positive side of their bad luck. And they also realize that they cannot sit around waiting for good things to happen; instead, they have to make them happen. Visualization can be key in realizing true wellth, but there's more to it than many people realize.

Visualization works if you work hard. That's the thing.
You can't just visualize and go eat a sandwich.

—JIM CARREY

My problem with a lot of self-help gurus is that they promote a message that is about entitlement. Yes, I truly believe that we all deserve a great life, a life filled with happiness, health, and abundance. But I also believe that this is a three-part process: believing, seeing, and doing. You can't just affirm, visualize, or pray and assume that what you want will magically transpire. And I think most religions actually back me up. Let me explain the process as I see it:

The first step is *believing*. You have to believe—otherwise you won't accomplish anything. If you don't believe you'll meet your soul mate, if you don't believe you'll get that raise, or if you don't believe you'll lose that weight, then it's over before you even start. It won't happen. Period.

I tend to think big and believe that huge things can happen. For example, when mindbodygreen launched out of our tiny apartment in Brooklyn, I envisioned it becoming an influential media brand that would make wellness accessible to the masses. I never saw it as a one-person blog. In fact, I corrected people when they said it was "just a blog." I saw it as something much bigger. I always believe in myself, and I also believe that anyone can accomplish anything that they set their minds to.

I'm a great believer in luck, and I find the harder I work, the more I have of it.

—F. L. EMERSON, *THE YALE BOOK OF QUOTATIONS*

If you have trouble believing in yourself—a key component of wellth—then start believing that you can accomplish little things. I'm not into repeating affirmations in the mirror, but I do believe in the power of words. Write down little goals, such as "I'm going to eat a healthy lunch that's filled with greens today." Think about it, too. What greens are you going to have? Kale or spinach or both? Will you have almonds or walnuts with your greens? What will the dressing taste like? Think about how great you're going to feel after eating such a healthy and delicious lunch. Then go fix your salad and enjoy it. You've just set out to accomplish something, and you did it.

Repeat your success with other small goals, eventually working your way up to bigger objectives. What you're doing is getting accustomed to accomplishing what you say out loud. That's a powerful and effective way to build self-confidence.

But let's say you've already got the believing part covered.

Next comes the importance of *seeing*. If you don't envision where you want to go, then how are you going to get from point A to point B? If you want to drive from New York to Los Angeles, you need to get a map or GPS to see how you're going to get there—otherwise you may wind up in Vancouver.

For example, if it's a soul mate you're looking for, you have to envision the person you're seeking—and not in terms of physical looks. You have to picture the qualities that are really important to you, and imagine the types of places where someone with those qualities would hang out. The same goes for weight loss, or starting a business, or practically anything. You need to see how you're going to get where you want to go. The plan doesn't have to be perfect, and quite often it will change, but you have to start by envisioning it.

The third step is *taking action*. You need to do what you set out to accomplish. If you're trying to lose weight, and you believe that you can lose twenty pounds, and you can see yourself walking for twenty minutes every day and cutting out sugar— well, now you have to actually start doing those things. Although weight loss is more about goal setting and less about luck, in some ways it's still about making your own luck. It involves changing how you see the world and thus how you change your life.

If you truly want to achieve a life filled with happiness, health, and abundance, these three principles are the keys to your success. Your behavior on the mat or at the gym (or at the office or the dinner table) affects your entire persona. So you're responsible for creating your own luck in every sense of the word and in every aspect of your life.

*You never know what worse luck your bad luck
has saved you from.*
—CORMAC MCCARTHY, *NO COUNTRY FOR OLD MEN*

—— Grow Your Life Savings: Believe ——

AVIVA ROMM, M.D., IS A Yale-trained, board-certified family physician, midwife, herbalist, and author. She has this to say about visualization:

Getting healthy requires making conscientious choices—but once you know how, it becomes a way of life. Too often, though, we quit before we've gotten very far, or we don't even start, because we don't believe that we can have the health that we desire.

The most difficult part of changing health is changing our beliefs. But once we do, the changes can last forever.

Most of us were taught that health was either something we had or didn't have—it's just in our genes, for example. We were not taught that it's something we have any control over. We tend to think negatively about our bodies and our ability to change. We hand our health over to experts. We focus on the obstacles, and often we get stuck. However, what happens in our minds has a tremendous influence over what happens in our bodies. Yet there is another way to think about—and create—health.

For instance, athletes visualize their success down to the specific details of their moves on the court or field.

- Bjorn Borg, the 1970s world champion tennis player, talked about mastering the perfect serve by visualizing it before he even tossed the ball into the air.
- Jack Nicklaus, world champion golfer, said, "I never hit a shot, not even in practice, without having a very sharp in-focus picture of it in my head."
- Mary Lou Retton, the first American to win the all-around gold medal in the Olympic Games, said in an interview with *Time* magazine that on the night before the finals in women's gymnastics, she lay in bed mentally rehearsing her performance.
- Gabby Douglas, another Olympic Gold–winning gymnast, also used this tool. "I visualized the floor set I wanted to do, and then I went out and hit the best floor routine of my life. It proved to me just how powerful my mind can be."

Becoming healthy requires that we believe in ourselves, and create new thought patterns that lead to sustainable practices. We do this by visualizing our success, just like world-class athletes.

Getting healthy requires us to actually see ourselves as healthy (or fit or slimmer or sleeping better, or fill-in-the-blank) before we even get there. We have to think ourselves well. It's a form of emotional fitness and mental retraining. The first time you do this, give yourself up to twenty minutes to really envision the dream you want to create. After that, you can do this practice in two minutes each day and get a lifetime of benefit!

Here are the steps:

- Find a quiet, comfortable place to relax for twenty minutes. Have a notebook and pen in hand, or your favorite electronic writing device. Make sure you've blocked out all distractions—cell phone, kids, partner, e-mail. You want to focus.
- Close your eyes and take four deep breaths—inhale deeply, exhale deeply.
- Now identify the goal you want to create. Be really detailed and specific about it—imagine the sensation you feel having accomplished your goal, and envision your surroundings. Think about what you're wearing, what you see, what you smell, how your friends and loved ones respond to the changes you've made. Imagine that it's already happening.
- Imagine that you're incredibly proud of yourself. You are positively glowing!
- Capture this image in your mind's eye. (Write it all down, too, so you don't forget!)
- Repeat this for several minutes every day.
- Reinforce your new practice with the following affirmations:

I am amazing.
I can do anything.
I am prepared to succeed.

Make sure to call up this image when making specific health choices; for example, when deciding between that muffin or veggies and hummus, or when you're torn between going for a quick run or getting glued to Facebook.

Don't hesitate to use visualization when you're making changes for your health. In fact, the more often you envision your goal, the closer it is to becoming a reality!

A QUICK DEPOSIT IN YOUR WELLTH ACCOUNT

- Only with hindsight are we able to see that things have worked out for the best in our lives. We have to connect the dots backward.
- No matter how bleak things can seem, try to know that God/the universe is watching out for you. We have to work hard while at the same time have faith and let go, trusting that something or someone has our backs.
- Lucky people are able to see the positive side of their bad luck. They realize that with time, what seems unlucky can turn out to be an opportunity.
- Visualization has three components: believing, seeing, and doing. You won't accomplish your goals without practicing all three.

CHAPTER 5

Explore

ON THE ROAD TO TOTAL wellth, we may have to take some detours. And that's not a bad thing, as long as it's done in the spirit of exploration. There can be many zigzags along the way to accomplishing your vision of excellence in your life and work. It helps to keep in mind that rarely is the path straight to success in either area. If we can have the fortitude to learn from the speed bumps and periods of stalling out, we can reach our goals with more knowledge and resilience than those who have had an easier road.

If you put off everything until you're sure of it, you'll never get anything done.

—NORMAN VINCENT PEALE, *THE POWER OF POSITIVE THINKING*

Throughout college and high school, I had a lot of odd, and crappy, jobs. Some were fun, and some were not so fun. In the latter category, I was a busboy and a dishwasher, and I worked at a moving and storage company. I also delivered beer, worked the counter at a delicatessen, and served fast food at a pool. My other jobs included being a bouncer, a deejay, and a bartender. One summer I worked security for the Democratic Party, and I even got to drive in a presidential motorcade. I also stood on corners and handed out flyers to get out the vote for campaigns.

Let me start with the worst and probably the most eye-opening job. The summer before my freshman year at Columbia University, I worked as a busboy at a local yacht club. It was like a scene out of *Caddyshack* but worse. There was a guy who was a dead ringer for Ted Knight's character, Judge Smails. He even wore the same captain's hat. The only problem with this real-life version of *Caddyshack* was there was no Rodney Dangerfield or Chevy Chase to lighten things up. Before I get too deeply into the type of people who belong to a yacht club, let me explain why this job sucked—and also why it was such an incredible learning experience.

First of all, being a busboy is tough work. You're constantly leaning over people to pour water, take dishes, or do whatever grunt work there is. And trying to guess when people are finished with their meals isn't fun—especially at a country club. At a regular restaurant, they want to turn the tables often, as the owners want to seat more people in order to drive revenue. So the faster you can bus a table and turn it over, the better.

Making money isn't hard in itself . . . What's hard is to earn it doing something worth devoting one's life to.

—CARLOS RUIZ ZAFÓN, *THE SHADOW OF THE WIND*

But in a country club, the opposite is true. Members and their guests just want to sit there all night, socialize, and be seen. They don't want to leave, because they have nowhere else to go. There's no incentive to turn tables. People linger all night, so having to wait in order to clear their plates is torturous. All you want to do as a busboy is clear plates and turn the table—but these tables never turned. It was the dinner that just went on and on, so you could never quite get your job done. Oh, and the policy of the club on tipping was that waiters didn't have to share tips. So they didn't. These are the reasons why I quit after just two long weeks.

Here's what I learned: I hate snobs. People in that club treated the waitstaff like second-class citizens. Many of the waiters and waitresses had emigrated from Mexico, and I learned how hard those workers had it. A group of ten or so of them actually lived at the club in tiny, god-awful quarters. They saved every penny to send back home to their families. Here I was a white kid who absolutely hated the job (and the people I was working for), but I had the power to quit at any moment. They had no choice whatsoever; this job was their life.

Johnnie was one of the workers. His English wasn't very good, but he worked extremely hard. One Saturday night we had been busing some guy's fiftieth-birthday dinner. The meal just went on and on as the whole group got more and more intoxicated. Around midnight, Johnnie asked if I could cover for him, as he had to go to his other job at a bagel store—which started at four a.m.! This twenty-five-year-old guy's life involved going from one crappy job busing tables for a bunch of snobs at midnight, to grinding away at a bagel store just four hours later. Boy, did that make me realize how lucky I was.

This country club gig, and all my other hospitality jobs (bartending, busing tables, bouncing), taught me a lot about people and the working world in general. I learned that most of these jobs are really hard. You're on your feet, busting your ass, and customers can be both incredibly cheap and incredible jerks. Once I waited on a woman who demanded that she be able to order a half-order of French fries at a pool snack bar. She also wanted to pay half the price. When I said I couldn't accommodate her request, she ranted, "Kids today can't make decisions!" I found it a bit humorous because I did make a decision, and the decision was not to give her a half-order.

But some customers can be amazingly kind. I'll never forget all the supergenerous tippers that I encountered while bartending. These guys and gals always showed up with a smile on their faces, along with a please and thank you—and they always left a good tip.

People in service positions are the folks who make our lives possible. We run into them everywhere we go: getting coffee, commuting, or checking out at the grocery line. The folks who wait on us, take our money, and help us get to our destinations are the backbone of our daily lives. They work so hard, and they don't make a lot of money doing things that make our lives convenient. So the least we can do is be kind and generous to them, every chance we get.

Working in the service industry taught me some incredible life lessons, which have made me a better entrepreneur and CEO. One lesson that I bring with me to work every day is the idea that no job is too small. Even though we have dozens of employees, I still take out the trash at our office, and pride myself on doing so.

When you dance, your purpose is not to get to a certain place on the floor. It's to enjoy each step along the way.

—WAYNE DYER, *THE ESSENTIAL WAYNE DYER COLLECTION*

Master the Art of Living

MANY PEOPLE, ESPECIALLY THOSE OF us who live in New York City, had a post-9/11 period of reflection or revisiting of their lives. For me, as I briefly discussed earlier in the book, the tragedy called into question my life on Wall Street. Engines full throttle, I'd been driving on that highway for three years. Like most traders, I worked furiously during the week and then walked out the door on Friday, burned out and ready to forget it all with a weekend of partying.

I didn't suddenly decide that I hated trading, but at a deep level, I knew I was done. I felt like I have toward the end of other relationships: we could hang on and try to make it work, but words had been exchanged and actions taken that altered it forever. Making money for money's sake just wasn't doing it for me anymore.

Then I came across a quote in an inspirational book that I often turned to when I was feeling down or lost. Lawrence Pearsall Jacks wrote in *Education through Recreation*:

A master in the art of living makes little distinction between his work and his play, his labor and his leisure, his mind and his body, his education and his recreation, his love and his religion. He hardly knows which is which. He simply pursues his vision of excellence through whatever he does, leaving others to decide whether he is working or playing. To him, he is always doing both.

When I read this, I knew immediately that I needed to leave the trading life. More than that, I knew I wanted to be a master in the art of living, even though I didn't know what form it would take or even what that meant. I did know that I wanted to experience a sense of alignment between who I was and my work, so that my work and life goals would blend and complement each other.

It took me almost ten years to fully get there, and it was a far-from-straight line. There were many starts, stops, and zig-zags along the way, but eventually I arrived at a good place. I wouldn't call myself a master, but now I genuinely play while I work, and work while I play. And every day when I wake up, I feel that I'm pursuing my personal vision of excellence.

A man is a success if he gets up in the morning and goes to bed at night, and in between does what he wants to do.

—BOB DYLAN

How I got to where I am now is a story of gradual awakening, tons of mistakes, and an eventual alignment of my actions with who I was becoming. It's not a "rags-to-riches" story but one that moves from being not at all well-off to a place of genuine abundance, far more treasure-filled than material wealth.

When I left Wall Street in 2002, I thought I had a big enough financial cushion to allow me to find my true vocation. So I began opening my eyes to other opportunities outside of trading. I decided I wanted the freedom and adventure of being an entrepreneur; that seemed like the right path to Lawrence Jacks's vision.

As it happened, friends of mine on the trading desk were investing in a health care startup. These buddies were some of the smartest people I knew. The company's financials were strong, the investment thesis seemed sound, and I believed that their product was a contribution to the field. I sank serious money into the company, confident that it would pay off. But it didn't, to put it mildly. I left the company only a few months after joining it, and eventually it folded.

The whole effort had been an exercise in hubris. My buddies and I weren't even close to being experts on health care. If we had been, at least some of the problems the company ran up against would have been apparent at the outset. Through this flop, I learned a valuable albeit expensive business lesson. It doesn't matter how smart you are, if you're analyzing a business about which you actually know little.

This is my problem with some MBAs—you can do all the case studies in the world and run numbers until you're blue in the face, but there's no substitute for knowledge and real-world experience. I also learned that entrepreneurship wasn't just about taking risks toward a payoff: it was about digging in, putting in sweat equity, and caring enough to become an expert *before* investing in a project. I had received an education, no doubt, but I had no idea what the next step was.

The health care company had brought me to Washington,

D.C., where I was keen on staying until I figured out what the hell I was going to do with my life. I went back to trading, this time from my apartment, and only often enough to pay the bills. In fact, I felt as if I were unlearning everything I'd learned on Wall Street. I didn't feel at all driven to succeed monetarily, to compete, to win the pot of gold.

Instead, I allowed myself to feel lost and unsure. I believed that if I put myself out there in the world, I would find a place to land. I volunteered at churches and soup kitchens. I interned on Capitol Hill. I spent countless hours in the self-help section of Barnes & Noble. One afternoon while browsing the religion aisle, I came across another quote that moved me deeply.

> Imagine yourself as a living house. God comes in to rebuild that house. At first, perhaps, you can understand what He is doing. He is getting the drains right and stopping the leaks in the roof and so on; you know that those jobs needed doing and so you're not surprised. But presently He starts knocking the house about in a way that hurts abominably and does not seem to make any sense. What on earth is He up to? The explanation is that He is building quite a different house from the one you thought of—throwing out a new wing here, putting on an extra floor there, running up towers, making courtyards. You thought you were being made into a decent little cottage: but He is building a palace. He intends to come and live in it Himself.

When I read this quote from *Mere Christianity* by C. S. Lewis, I felt rumblings and a kind of yearning. It affirmed my intuition that I needed to surrender to whatever was unfolding rather than trying to make it happen. It also enlivened my sense of possibility. I wanted a palace in which I felt connected both to myself and to a purpose larger than myself.

The answer? Cheesecake. I was fit and thriving on a low-carb, low-sugar diet, but cheesecake had always been my dessert kryptonite. It was the only thing I knew how to bake, and I did it well, thanks to my grandmother who'd taught me. It was my contribution to every holiday meal. Every time I baked one, I felt a connection to someone who'd meant the world to me. For me, cheesecake was about love.

I decided that cheesecake was my future. But not just any cheesecake: a low-carb one. Low-sugar, low-carb diets were catching on in a big way. And as I was thriving on that diet, I wanted to be part of the trend. I thought a low-carb cheesecake would be the perfect indulgence for sweets-deprived dieters. I hadn't known anything about health care—but I knew cheesecakes! In addition, I was excited to educate myself about the exploding natural products market. Two years after my first failed startup, I put my foot back in the water. Soon I was completely submerged.

I began selling cheesecakes and went from a business focused on retail distribution to an e-commerce business. But ultimately I had to close it down. I had spent another three years striving toward something meaningful but with not much to show for it, except some excellent lessons in what *not* to do.

This one hurt. I had poured my heart and soul (and my money) into a business that had real meaning to me. I believed in it so much that I'd stopped the little trading I had been doing to get by. I could have gone back to trading, but I felt strongly that it was a crutch, one that I had to kick or I'd never go all in as an entrepreneur.

So at the age of thirty, I sucked it up and moved back home to live with my mom and grandma. I couldn't believe that I'd joined the legions of young adults moving back home. Two years later, I was still living there.

I like money, but it's never been about the money.

—JERRY SEINFELD

During this time, I felt like a loser—a taller, more athletic version of George Costanza from *Seinfeld*. Other times I'd get energized enough to network with an old high school or Columbia friend. Occasionally, I'd meet with people who seemed charged up about their jobs or businesses. I knew that as badly as I wanted an income, I needed to feel as charged up as they were before I made my next move. Just as important, I wanted to have a partner, someone to brainstorm with and to help me weather the hardships that accompanied every new business venture.

At a certain point, I decided to stop being hard on myself, to let go and be low profile for a while longer, and let things unfold. I'm a pretty hard-driving guy, and yet when things go sour, you now know from these pages, I have always believed that it would all work out. I know that this has been a key to my entrepreneurial fortitude—accepting failure, pausing, and then moving on. Goals and deadlines are important, but sometimes you just have to say, "I don't know when, I don't know how, but I know it's gonna happen."

Aligning Your Values and Passion

AFTER MY FAILED CHEESECAKE BUSINESS and another venture that involved organic cookies, I began to see that the arena of wellness was where my heart was. (Yes, it's a bit ironic that cookies ultimately led me to become passionate about organics and the environment.) I wanted to be a part of this larger world and make some kind of contribution. More specifically, I wanted to bring what I had begun to learn about food, the environment, and yoga to an audience of people like me, on their road to self-discovery. For the first time since I'd set out on my entrepreneurial path, I felt that the C. S. Lewis and Lawrence Jacks quotes were beginning to come to fruition in my life. My foundation was being completely rebuilt, and I could see how my personal and professional passions might intersect.

I also knew that whatever I did next would not be about one product. I never wanted to ship boxes or hold inventory again. I've always thought that the best way to spread ideas and make change was through media. That was where I wanted to be. I didn't know what exactly my new business would be, but I had a name, mindbodygreen. And I felt my vision starting to emerge. I imagined a website devoted to health and happiness that would be inspiring, informative, and entertaining. That was a good enough beginning for me.

The story of mindbodygreen is far from over. In fact, I think we haven't even scratched the surface. I believe that we and all our contributors, readers, and viewers are creating a powerful wellness movement from the ground up. My deepest hope is that this movement, and in some small way this book, will inspire people to pursue their own definition of happiness, health, and wellth—not the kind that comes overnight, but the kind that seeps gently into your life and stays forever.

Although I'm a big believer in merging values and passion in the workplace, the reality is that this isn't always an option for everyone. If it isn't an option for you, then I suggest you build your passions into your life through everything you do outside work—whether it's your hobbies, your travel, your family . . . anything. Sometimes it seems as if people who are able to merge passion with their jobs are just lucky, but I believe that often you can make your own luck.

How to Create Your Own Luck

WHAT IS LUCK? IS IT fate? Is it chance? Is it the gods smiling down upon you? Guess again, says Dr. Richard Wiseman, author of *The Luck Factor.* After three years of research, Wiseman arrived at the conclusion that luck can actually be learned. He breaks down the concept of luckiness into four principles.

Maximize Chance Opportunities: Lucky people create, notice, and act upon the chance opportunities in their lives. With regard to business, I believe that this principle is the key to success. You really have to maximize opportunities and make things happen. Sometimes these opportunities amount to nothing, and sometimes they can change the course of your life. But you'll never know for sure if you don't do anything. At least you'll know you gave yourself a shot. As Hall of Fame hockey player Wayne Gretzky once said, "You miss 100 percent of the shots you don't take."

Listen to Your Hunches: Lucky people make successful decisions by using their intuition and gut feelings. We all have gut feelings, and we should pay attention to them.

Expect Good Fortune: Lucky people's expectations about the future help them fulfill their dreams and ambitions.

Turn Bad Luck into Good: Lucky people have the ability to see the positive side of their bad luck.

There Are No Shortcuts

HERE'S THE THING ABOUT FINDING your calling: you still have to do the grunt work. I believe that very few people know what their calling is at a young age, or when they first get out of college. Typically those who do find their calling early on are creatives or athletes, people filled with so much passion for their vocation that it's literally all they can think about doing.

This is extremely rare. For most people, doing the grunt work is essential in the process of finding your calling. It's through those early jobs out of high school or college that you figure out what you're good at, what you're bad at, and more important, what you like and dislike. I've found that oftentimes there's a disconnect between your *perception* of what a job entails and its reality.

There are two primary choices in life: to accept conditions as they exist, or accept the responsibility for changing them.

—DENIS WAITLEY, *BEING THE BEST*

For example, when I was in Washington, D.C., I had an idea that working on Capitol Hill would be very exciting, with lots of wheeling and dealing, as in *House of Cards*. But the reality is, it wasn't. Instead, the job requirements were centered on wordsmithing and document reading, blended with lots of networking. It was not nearly as exciting as Kevin Spacey leads you to believe! Or at least not at the intern level.

You have to be patient when it comes to finding your passion. For me, it took years and years. I think your twenties are all about working very hard and learning and building skills, while taking an inventory of what you like and don't like—essentially, figuring out who you are. In your thirties, you start to know who you are, and you can begin to build a life or a career around your identity. In your forties, you can try to hone your career focus so it's more closely aligned with your passion.

Yet you don't have to drop your day job to do this. You

can begin to follow your passion, or to build the life you want, after office hours. My wife, Colleen, is just as passionate about wellness as I am. She wrote blog posts, and did just about anything I needed her help with, at night or on the weekends when mindbodygreen had only one full-time employee—me. My incredible cofounders Tim and Carver did the same thing, keeping their day jobs and writing code after six p.m. and on weekends.

There is no passion to be found playing small—in settling for a life that is less than the one you are capable of living.

—NELSON MANDELA, *LONG WALK TO FREEDOM*

Your passion doesn't have to be running or starting a company. Your passion could be eating at great restaurants, hanging out with friends, or traveling—that's great. If that's the case, then I suggest building a life that allows you to do those things. I believe that everyone can follow their passion; we just need to explore what our passions really are.

—— Grow Your Life Savings: Explore ——

I'VE BEEN INSPIRED BY FELLOW entrepreneur Joe Cross, whose hit documentary, *Fat Sick & Nearly Dead,* tracked his journey to being—as he puts it—"100 pounds lighter and 1,000 times happier." Below are seven principles that he learned on the road to wellth. They're so aligned with my own that I have to share them.

1. **Listen for what calls to you.** Allow it to emerge from your personal needs and desires for yourself and the world, even if what is calling you may make no sense at first. You may just surprise yourself with what you do next.

2. **Doubt is normal,** but don't let it gain momentum. Consciously cancel it out with your belief in what you are doing.

3. **Trust others, but not naïvely.** Know what you don't know, and find the experts who can make up for your shortcomings. Once you find them, value and trust them.

4. **Follow your plan and see it through,** but be aware that it will usually take twice as long, and cost twice as much as you think it will.

5. **Don't be afraid to make a fool of yourself.** Even if it means publicly failing.

6. There is likely a career path that would make you far more money, but I can attest that **money really doesn't buy happiness.** Health and helping others does.

7. And remember, any **success takes a certain amount of luck.** Don't mistake your luck for your genius. And be thankful for the luck that comes your way.

A QUICK DEPOSIT IN YOUR WELLTH ACCOUNT

- Working grubby summer jobs can be a great way to learn a lot about people and life. Don't consider any job beneath you; instead, think of it as a learning experience.
- In order to follow your passion, you first need to define what it is. Only then can you go after your dreams.
- Be patient about finding your passion; it can take years. And you don't have to quit your day job in order to find it.
- Become a master in the art of living who makes little distinction between work and play, labor and leisure.

CHAPTER 6

Breathe

THE MIND-BODY CONNECTION IS ONE of the pillars of wellth—and meditation is a cornerstone. But the thought of meditation makes some people cringe as they think that they'll never be able to do it because they can't concentrate, or they don't have time, or they have a "monkey mind." This is all misinformation. As long as you can breathe, you can meditate. That's it. And it's that simple. Even though I've meditated on and off for the past few years, I recently got serious about incorporating it into my daily routine. Why now? In living "mindbodygreen," I felt that I'd been doing a pretty good job with the body and the green, whereas I didn't have a consistent practice for my mind.

> *You can't stop the waves, but you can learn to surf.*
> —JON KABAT-ZINN, *WHEREVER YOU GO, THERE YOU ARE*

At our "revitalize" event in summer of 2014, author and news anchor Dan Harris made clear that it's just as important to exercise the mind as it is the body. After hearing him speak, I decided that I needed to make a change before my fortieth birthday. So for over a year now, I've been meditating twice a day for twenty minutes at a time, once in the morning and once in the afternoon or evening. I've been pretty good about being consistent; even though sometimes I miss a session, I rarely miss a day.

Suffice it to say that I'm totally hooked. I feel like a mental fog lifts from my brain after each session. I feel more relaxed. I'm calmer. I'm more in tune with my inner sense of knowing than ever before. I experience more coincidences. I also *feel* more intensely; if I'm happy, I feel almost ecstatic; or if I'm eating one of my favorite dishes, it seems to taste even better than I remembered.

Since I got serious about maintaining a daily meditation practice, it's as if I went from experiencing my life through a black-and-white TV to experiencing it through HDTV with satellite—sharper, with color, and more channels! It's my new favorite tool in my ever-growing health and happiness tool kit, and I hope that you'll try it. In the morning, I'll brush my teeth and then sit on my bed and meditate for twenty minutes before I have coffee and breakfast. In the late afternoon, I'll sneak away into one of our conference rooms and meditate in there for twenty minutes. If that doesn't work out timewise, I'll meditate at home before dinner.

And you don't have to spend hours meditating; you can receive benefits from only five minutes per day. Some who practice the mindfulness form of meditation, where you concentrate on specific objects, your breathing, or parts of your body, meditate on their daily commute on the bus or train.

Mindfulness helps you go home to the present.
And every time you go there and recognize a condition
of happiness that you have, happiness comes.
—THICH NHAT HANH, *ANGER: WISDOM FOR COOLING THE FLAMES*

Create a Calming Space

IF YOU MEDITATE AT HOME or simply want a more conducive atmosphere for relaxation, consider the feeling/energy that you have created in your living space. You know the sensation when you walk into a spa or a resort and immediately you feel relaxed or Zen-like? That is no accident; in fact, that impression was created intentionally. I'm a huge believer in making your space work for you. Whether it's your home or office, you need the optimal setup for work, play, or relaxation. And there's an art to it.

One simple concept is to clear away clutter. Get rid of the old to make room for the new, and remember that a cluttered desk can equate to a cluttered mind. I don't think you necessarily need a big home and lots of money to create a space that serves you instead of drains you. For instance, Colleen and I have a few simple practices such as placing candles around our apartment, putting up pictures of loved ones, and not piling up a lot of junk—especially old clothes. If we don't wear something for six months, then we give it to Goodwill. We also don't buy a lot of stuff for our home. We've found that we're much happier when we try to keep it simple.

My friend Dana Claudat, a feng shui expert, has a few tips to help anyone make their home more of a sanctuary:

Turn off bright lights and electronics at least an hour before bed. Keeping them low whenever possible creates a calmer and more receptive space.

Texture is huge! Use throw blankets or extra pillows in your living area or bedroom. Even soft slippers can make all the difference if you have very hard or cold floors.

Adjust temperature. If you're too hot or cold, either will be stressful to your system. Do your best to regulate room temperatures so they don't run to extremes.

Remove anything you don't like or is negative. You may not really pay attention to everything that's in your home, such as the painting or print that you don't really like, and you keep it up just to have something on your walls. Don't! And clutter is an obvious negative message that can go!

Light up. Simple aromatherapy candles like those made from lavender essential oils will make your space more relaxing physically and emotionally.

Give yourself a "you space," be it a bunch of floor pillows, altar, or a corner—a space where you can meditate, have your coffee or tea, or simply just kick back.

Stick to nature. Bring a feeling of nature to your home with plants and earthy materials like pottery or even crystals.

I have found that all these tips work. It doesn't matter if you live in a three-hundred-square-foot studio or a three-thousand-square-foot house. Anyone can do all of the above immediately, at little or no cost.

Does this spark joy? If it does, keep it.
If not, dispose of it.
—MARIE KONDO, *THE LIFE-CHANGING MAGIC OF TIDYING UP*

The Mind-Body Connection

NOW THAT I'M EMBEDDED IN the wellness world, I've truly seen the power of what my friend Dr. Lissa Rankin calls "mind over medicine" (also the title of her best-selling book). In the book, Lissa shares some incredible anecdotes about the mind's power to heal—and also to hurt. One story that stood out for me was "The Blind Women of Khmer Rouge."

As described in Anne Harrington's *The Cure Within*, 200 cases of blindness were reported in a group of Cambodian women forced by the Khmer Rouge to witness the torture and slaughter of those close to them, particularly the men in their lives. Examination of these women found nothing physically wrong with their eyes. The conclusion those trying to help them came to was that by being forced to view the unbearable, "they had all cried until they could not see."

Wow. If that's not a powerful story about stress, then I don't know what is. I wholeheartedly believe that it's not a sickness or injury that does us in. Instead, it's the stress surrounding that injury that makes it worse. But how can you not be upset when something catastrophic, even perhaps life-threatening, is wrong with you? How are you supposed to avoid feeling stressed about it?

What I've learned is that whenever you're not feeling well, or you're faced with a health issue that's serious, you should try to believe that you're going to heal. Believe that no matter how long the healing process takes, or even if it doesn't improve or your condition worsens, eventually you will be okay.

Your Mind Wags Your Body

YOUR BODY DOESN'T CONTROL YOUR mind. Instead, your mind directs your body. This statement isn't New Age propaganda—science supports it.

The scariest day of my life was May 21, 2012. I'm sure Colleen would agree. I was working out of our apartment in Brooklyn, getting ready to load all the mindbodygreen Facebook posts for the day. Colleen had an appointment with her doctor in Manhattan before she headed to work in midtown. When I picked up the phone on that crisp spring morning, I immediately sensed that something was very wrong. Colleen was crying and could barely talk. If you've ever experienced a moment like that, when a loved one calls and you don't know why they're in such distress, you know that it's absolutely awful. It's as if time stops—an ellipsis of worry inserted into an eternity.

Colleen uttered the words, "I'm going to the emergency room. They think I have a pulmonary embolism." My mind racing, I took a deep breath and said, "You're going to be okay. I love you, and you're going to be okay. I'm going to the hospital now." I shut my laptop.

Then as I ran to hail a cab, I called my mom to tell her what had happened. She said, "Grandma is watching over her. Colleen will be okay." It was just a few weeks after my grandmother had passed away. Surely God wouldn't take away my wife after I'd just lost my grandmother? Could He be so cruel? I didn't think so, but at that moment I didn't have time to think; I was just running on adrenaline.

I got into a cab and made it to NYU Hospital from Brooklyn faster than Colleen had from SoHo. I didn't know I'd beaten her there, and I couldn't get hold of her, so when I didn't see her, I began to get worried. I thought, "Did she not make it to the hospital? Is she lying unconscious in a taxi?" Frantically, I ran to another entrance and asked if she had checked in, but they said no. I ran back to the first entrance, where Colleen was just pulling up in her cab.

For a moment I breathed a sigh of relief. Then we were ushered in, and Colleen went through all the testing you'd expect. At the same time, I was Googling everything I could find on pulmonary embolisms. First I found that Serena Williams had had one, and next I read that they can kill you. Everything I read was terrifying.

The first question the doctor asked was "Were you on a flight recently?" We had flown back from Miami a week earlier.

Colleen also had a leg cramp that wouldn't go away and that had gotten worse. I had insisted that she see her doctor that morning because she had been abnormally tired, was coughing, and even had some trouble breathing; all are symptoms that scream "pulmonary embolism" if you know what to look for. Next they asked if she was on the Pill. She was.

After more tests and an X-ray, they concluded that Colleen indeed had a pulmonary embolism. The doctor said that she had so much clotting, she was lucky she didn't have a stroke and die. It was a close call. We lay side by side in a tiny hospital bed that night, but each of us barely slept. We held each other tightly. If I hadn't insisted that Colleen go see her doctor that morning, it's likely she would have died.

The next day Colleen's sister Kerry came by to see us with her fiancé (now husband) Eric, as well as our friends Tara Stiles and Michael Taylor. Colleen was discharged later that afternoon, and she would have to take blood thinners for a while. The prognosis wasn't bad, considering what could have happened.

It was possible that a miracle was not something that happened to you, but rather something that didn't.

—JODI PICOULT, *THE TENTH CIRCLE*

But then the *why* began—as it should, after almost losing your life. Colleen underwent a lot of medical tests to figure out why she'd had an embolism. The Pill definitely contributed, especially since the one she was taking had an increased chance of causing clotting. It's funny how even women who are obsessed with health often don't check out the small print about the Pill. There are real risks, but most overlook them. Suffice it to say, Colleen stopped taking the Pill and will never go back on it again.

After all the testing, the doctors couldn't really figure out why she had had an embolism, and we still don't know. And after ditching the Pill, it took Colleen almost three years to get her period again. But as with any health crisis, there were two sides to it: the medical and the spiritual. Western medicine didn't have answers that satisfied either of us. Colleen's dad experienced a blood clot while climbing Mount Everest, which put Colleen at a higher risk. But after all the genetic testing to determine if this was purely hereditary, doctors didn't draw any real conclusions and were left puzzled. So if we weren't getting insight from modern medicine, what could spirituality tell us about why this had happened?

In an effort to find some answers, Colleen reread Louise Hay's classic self-help book, *You Can Heal Your Life*. Hay believes that most illness is due to anger and stress. She also believes we have the power to heal anything ourselves, just by changing our belief system. Neither Colleen nor I necessarily agree with this type of thinking, but I do believe that there's a powerful connection between the mind and body that we do not yet fully comprehend. Hay feels that she overcame cancer this way. She's a big believer in affirmations, which for me are a bit much. Standing in front of a mirror and repeating "I am radiant" isn't exactly my cup of tea, either. But I also know lots of successful people who swear by them.

You have the power to heal your life, and you need to know
that. We think so often that we are helpless, but we're not.
We always have the power of our minds. . . . Claim and
consciously use your power.

—LOUISE HAY, *YOU CAN HEAL YOUR LIFE*

Hay's book includes a list of various ailments, along with the spiritual root cause. This information really resonated with me, as blood clots went along with a reduction in the "joy of life," which really hit home. At the time, Colleen was working at a soul-crushing job with ridiculous hours and no personal fulfillment whatsoever.

Even more startling was an astrology reading later in which the astrologist told Colleen that around the day she had the embolism, she had experienced a cosmic wake-up call. Colleen and I aren't really into astrology, but the day of the reading, we were convinced there was something to it. She indeed got that wake-up call and decided to leave her job. Eventually she followed her passion for wellness and joined me at mindbodygreen. To this day, we don't have answers as to why she had the embolism (even after comprehensive genetic testing). But we definitely believe that stress played a role. We don't look to astrologists or to Louise Hay for our primary medical advice, and we don't recommend that anyone do this, but we both found these coincidences interesting. Sometimes life's greatest lessons can be the scariest and most painful. And sometimes there are no good answers to *why* something terrible happened. Yet the mind and the spirit are more powerful than you can imagine. I don't need to watch anyone die, or almost die, again, to be convinced of that. I know that if I can take the time to breathe, meditate, and reduce stress, I can deal with painful experiences with more equanimity.

—— Grow Your Life Savings: Breathe ——

GETTING STARTED WITH MEDITATION IS a lot easier than you think. My good friend and meditation teacher Charlie Knoles provides four simple steps to get started today.

1. **Sit.** Start by sitting comfortably, whatever that means to you. If you've practiced yoga for twenty years and lived in a Buddhist monastery studying Zen, please feel free to sit on a rock in lotus position. You've earned it. For everyone else, you can just sit in a chair or on your bed with a cushion behind you and keeping your spine straight. It doesn't matter if your legs are crossed or out in front of you. As long as you're upright and comfortable, you'll do fine.

2. **Breathe.** Bring your attention to your breath. Focus on your exhales, and make them really long. Breathe out the way you would if you just got into a nice warm bath on a freezing-cold day (or just stepped into an air-conditioned room on a sweltering-hot day). Your inhales should stay their normal length. Long exhales, shorter inhales. When you first begin, you will probably be able to breathe out for about twice as long as you breathe

in. Perhaps it's an inhale for a count of two and an exhale for a count of four. See if it feels comfortable to exhale a little longer. Maybe the exhale becomes a count of six, eight, or even more. If you feel short of breath, just breathe normally for a few breaths, and then return to the longest exhale that felt comfortable. It's not a competition. You're just finding out where your point of comfort is, and then staying there.

3. **Let go.** Now that you've set up this nice pattern in your breathing, stop trying to control your breath and just observe it. Your breath may even out; it might get deeper; it might get quicker or slower. Just watch it. If other thoughts come into your mind, just notice them and then return to observing your breath.

4. **Repeat.** Congratulations! You just did your first meditation. That wasn't so hard, was it? Now try it again tomorrow. You'll find that the more you do it the easier it becomes to relax into. If you stop practicing, you'll start from square one again, so it makes sense to do it every day and become an expert at deeply relaxing. You'll notice that you can do this little sequence for any length of time. Start with five minutes and if that feels easy, move up to ten minutes. From there, you can meditate longer if you like.

You might have noticed that I didn't say anything about closing your eyes. As a beginner, you'll probably find it easier to sit with your eyes closed to reduce distractions. But as you get more experienced, you'll be able to do this exercise anytime you need a bit more calm and presence. I was actually following my own instructions while I was typing, and now I feel great. I do a seated, eyes-closed, meditation twice a day, but I find that I can give myself these lovely little bursts of calm and positive feelings by introducing an element of my meditative practice into my life. I do it whenever I have idle time; for example, when I'm working, sitting in traffic, or waiting in line.

A QUICK DEPOSIT IN YOUR WELLTH ACCOUNT

- The mind-body connection is extremely powerful and far-reaching, and can extend to healing.
- Meditation can reduce stress, help you sleep better, improve the immune system, and increase concentration.
- Meditation can bring about true personal transformation.
- Believe that you can heal yourself, find the right support, listen to your body and diagnose the issue, write the prescription, and surrender attachment to the outcome.

CHAPTER 7

Feel

EMOTIONAL HEALTH IS A KEY aspect of overall wellth. Even if we don't have physical issues, we can't be healthy unless our psychological state mirrors our body's wellness. In this chapter, I'll delve into some of the components of emotional well-being.

Social Connections Are Vital

HAVING EMOTIONAL AND SOCIAL CONNECTIONS is important to our well-being. Indeed, it's been proven that people live longer if they have a number of close friends. The Centre for Ageing Studies at Flinders University in Australia found that people with a large network of friends outlived those with the least number of friends by an average of 22 percent. A study cited in *Lancet* showed that women who had breast cancer and were in a support group lived twice as long as those who weren't in a group. Many other studies have revealed the importance of friendships not only to mental health but to physical health.

Feeling connected to people who support you emotionally, psychologically, and socially is a key aspect of wellth.

A social group can be defined as two or more people who interact with each other, have some of the same characteristics, and share a sense of unified purpose. In his book *Outliers*, Malcolm Gladwell talks about the power of social groups, as they play a large factor in the success of children. University of Oxford anthropologist and psychologist Robin Dunbar also provides interesting information on the power of social groups. After conducting a number of experiments, he came up with the concept of Dunbar's Number, actually several different numbers as they pertain to different social groups.

Looking at the size of the human brain, Dunbar concluded that the average person can have 150 people in their social group. (I don't think the people at Facebook like this idea!) These are your casual friends that you'd probably want to invite to a party. Dunbar believes that anything over that 150 is too many for the human brain to handle. The next number is 50, and these are the friends that you'd probably invite to a group dinner. The next number, 15, is intimate friends in whom you confide. Then there's your most intimate group, your five close friends who are your best friends. They're a huge influence on who you are and who you will become as a person.

As I mentioned, social groups can be an important aspect of emotional well-being. Yet hanging out with the wrong group can lead us astray. I've seen the power of social groups many times in my life—the good, the bad, and the ugly.

In the Pulitzer Prize–winning memoir *The Tender Bar*, J. R. Moehringer characterizes Manhasset, my hometown, as renowned for lacrosse, the Catholic Church, and booze. He was right on the money. Alcohol fueled the town. I've never seen so many high-functioning alcoholics in one place. It was very common to see people leaving the gigantic liquor store on the main road with shopping carts filled with booze, as if it were Costco.

People drank hard, and they drank often. And it started in high school. Everyone drank—I mean *everyone*. And we all drank a lot. The amount of alcohol we consumed was ridiculous. We even ran the numbers and realized that if more than six people were drinking, then it made financial sense to purchase a keg (165 beers!) because it was cheaper than buying six twelve-packs.

Although I was a serious athlete, drinking and partying were still my number-one priorities. I wasn't the life of the party, but I was definitely the guy who organized those evenings of debauchery and got everyone going.

Back then there were no cell phones, no e-mail, and no Facebook, so we'd often spend Saturday afternoons driving around town collecting money from everyone so we could buy kegs. This was my first experience in raising capital. I drove my mom's 1989 white Jeep Cherokee Laredo, and we'd pile in with just enough space in the back to fit five kegs of beer. The beer depot owner knew we were underage, but he likely didn't care since I had a fake ID, and at seventeen I could pass for twenty-one.

In the greater Manhasset area, there were five country clubs. In back of the clubhouses there were empty kegs, ripe for the taking. We worked out a plan where we could pick up empty kegs from country clubs without the clubs realizing it and turn them in for the ten-dollar deposit. No one ever noticed, and no one ever cared. That didn't make it right, but we didn't even think about its being dishonest. No one raised his hand and said, "Maybe this isn't a good idea. This is stealing." Everyone just went along with the idea. And not only two or three guys were in on it; there were about twenty. Talk about the power of social groups!

Something else we all did was cheat. We even had the master key that opened up classrooms so we could steal exams. This cheating went beyond just twenty people; it was practically our entire class of 153 students. The culture was so competitive, so tied up in grades and where we were going to college, that even the top students would do anything to improve their scores. It wasn't about the work or the process; it was about the finish line. Cheating was endemic. Even though it was totally wrong, you almost felt as if you had to cheat to stay competitive.

I take responsibility for my behavior; it's something I'm not proud of, especially as I often led the charge. But in the end, it burned me. My senior year I got caught cheating on a physics test, and my teacher gave me a big fat F. It was that F that killed my chances to play basketball at an Ivy League school and forced me to go do a postgraduate year at Northfield Mount Hermon (which eventually ended up being one of the best things that ever happened to me). But what had really pissed me off about the F was the fact that the teacher zeroed in on me. Practically the whole class was cheating, but she made an example of me. At the time, it didn't occur to me that it would never have happened if I hadn't been to blame.

So we stole and we cheated in high school. These were just some of the many bad choices that I and my social group made.

And here's an even more extreme example of bad behavior. I'll never forget the conversation I had with a friend of mine's father about when his son got a DWI and tried to lose a police car in a high-speed chase, before eventually getting pulled over and arrested.

Although I wasn't in the car that night, I knew the four other guys who were with him—and they all thought the chase was a great idea. They were cheering him on to "outrun the cop"! These well-educated guys went on to great colleges and became very successful. Yet in high school the influence of peer pressure made them do something incredibly stupid.

Fat, drunk, and stupid is no way to go through life, son.
—DEAN VERNON WORMER, *ANIMAL HOUSE*

Peer pressure can be extremely powerful. It doesn't take a bad person to influence others to make bad choices. In terms of social groups, decision making can be a slippery slope. Often it isn't one defining moment or decision that changes your life for better or worse but several small ones. As with reading a map while driving, you make a series of wrong turns that collectively add up to going so off course, you wind up in another country.

And sure, some of our behavior had to do with being young, testosterone-filled guys who were trying to be cool. But it also shows the power of social groups and how difficult it is not to go along with everyone else. It has nothing to do with being weak or strong; it's about fitting in. Feeling you're part of a group, feeling you belong, is one of our key needs—especially as teenagers.

But if social groups can lead to ridiculously unsafe and unethical high school and college misbehavior and mischief— which even led me to a night in a jail cell for drunk and disorderly conduct (it's never a good idea to attempt to steal a street sign)—they can also lead to incredibly powerful inspiration and change in adulthood. I've seen proof of this through mindbodygreen.

In the wellness community, I have met some of the most inspiring, healthy people in the world. Some of them have become my closest friends. Rather than a culture built around underachieving and partying, this friend group is built around true support. When you hang around people who think big, follow their passion, and are doing amazing things, it can't help but rub off. Numerous times, a dear friend or I have come up with a wild, big idea that most people would immediately frown at or poke holes in. But instead of that, we bounce ideas around and often take the concept to another level.

Through life events like marriage, work, and having kids, your social group does tend to get smaller. Rather than being a composite of the twenty people that you party with, as an adult you're a combination of the five people you hang out with the most. From time to time, it's a good idea to list those five people in your life and evaluate how they're affecting you.

Who do I spend most of my time with now, other than my wife? Who are the people that I choose (and *choose* is the key) to be around, who support me, inspire me, and bring out the best in me?

One of my good friends, who thinks bigger than anyone else, is Tara Stiles. Tara is one of the most successful and well-known personalities in the yoga community. Recently she visited our new, much larger office in the Dumbo section of Brooklyn. She easily could have said, "Wow, this must be really expensive. How are you paying for this? Are you nervous about making the rent?" Instead, she was happy for us. She said, "I'll bet you take over the whole building one day." While many people might have had a mixed reaction or even shot down our ideas, Tara was and is always upbeat.

Tara's husband, Michael, is also extremely supportive of our business efforts. He is one of the most thoughtful people I know—he's always asking how you're doing and always complimentary of how mindbodygreen is doing. He's the type of guy who no matter what's going on in your life, he's there to support you. He's genuinely passionate about helping people, and it shows in everything he does. Colleen and I hang out with Tara and Michael a lot. It's great to connect with another couple who shares the same values. We're also in business together, as Tara and Michael are investors in mindbodygreen. They're two of the most important of the five people with whom I surround myself.

I am also blessed to have an incredible sister-in-law with whom I spend a ton of time at work, as she's our founding editor-in-chief. What I love about Kerry is her big brain and her empathy. She's a genius when it comes to content, and she balances it with a healthy amount of skepticism. She's also one of the most empathetic people I know. She's an amazing listener and is incredibly kind to strangers. We definitely have a unique relationship; we often fight like siblings, yet she's more than a sister-in-law to me. She's a confidante, and I trust her immensely.

I've known John Derderian forever (since second grade). He was one of my best childhood friends, and although we both partook in a lot of high school hijinks, he has evolved into one of the smartest, most creative people I know. Currently he works at Netflix in L.A. Whenever we get together, it's a non-stop stream-of-consciousness talk about film, TV, books, news, culture, wellness, you name it. Months can go by without our talking to or seeing each other, but we always pick up right where we left off. John is incredibly supportive and filled with amazing ideas. After a catch-up session, I feel like the creative side of my brain just got a kick-start. Colleen thinks it's funny to watch us talk because we're on our own separate wavelength.

Last but certainly not least, the person I spend almost every waking minute with is my wife, Colleen. Unlike most couples who kiss each other goodbye in the morning, Colleen and I work together all day at mindbodygreen. And we don't strangle each other, either! Our passion is intertwined with mindbodygreen, as are our friends. Colleen often helps me to balance my thinking at home and at work, just like yin and yang. At home, she is always looking to explore—whether it's culture, arts, restaurants, or travel. And she inspires me to try new things. I have a tendency to be a creature of habit, but she gets me out of my comfort zone in a good way. Whether it's going to the Matisse exhibit at the Museum of Modern Art or traveling to Nashville, she encourages me to experience things that I'd normally balk at but end up loving.

I'll also extend my list to add my mother, because she is

the person I've spent more time with than anyone else over the course of my life. She has always made me feel loved and supported and that I could achieve anything I put my mind to. Not everyone has that, and her love and support at an early age hardwired me for success, to some degree. It's something that I don't take for granted, and for which I'm eternally grateful.

If I had to summarize each of the traits that these people share, it's a blend of curiosity, kindness, smarts, and a passion for learning. No one is a Debbie Downer; they're all can-do people who are accomplishing great things. Being around them makes me want to be a better person and shows me that life is truly full of infinite possibility.

Think about the five people in your own life who influence you the most. Are they passing on positive energy or negative? Do you feel better or worse after having been with them? Do they bring out the best in you or the opposite? If anyone is bringing you down, how can you spend less time around him or her and more time with someone who is more uplifting? You don't have to cut people out of your life overnight; you can simply fade them out over time. You'll find that this becomes easier the more you do it.

Don't walk behind me; I may not lead.
Don't walk in front of me; I may not follow.
Just walk beside me and be my friend.

—ANONYMOUS

Energy Is Palpable

HAVE YOU EVER BEEN AROUND friends or family members who always make you feel good? They don't make you feel good by flattering you or buying you things. Instead, they brighten your day just by being near. Whether it's the way they shake your hand, hug you, or simply sit in the room with you, they can elevate your mood. The feeling is almost indescribable, but it's what happens when we spend time with someone with whom we truly enjoy being.

The opposite happens when we're around people who give off negative energy. Everyone has felt that drained sensation after being around someone who's a drag on our spirits. It can be the negative words they speak; their sour, critical facial expression; or the black cloud that seems to hang over them even when something positive has occurred. Whatever the manner in which they express it, this type of person can sap our energy simply by being in the same room with us.

And there are positive types of energy, just as there are positive types of people. One of the reasons I love having our office in Brooklyn is that the creative energy in our section of Dumbo is palpable. With so many entrepreneurs and artists clustered in one place, it's as if ideas are in the air. It's a very different feeling from, say, midtown Manhattan, with its high-rises and stiff-looking people in suits. Here there's a vibe of stress, anger, and hurriedness. Walking around our neighborhood, you just feel the creative energy, which goes beyond dress codes and facial hair.

And then there's the energy that I feel whenever I get together with my buddies, particularly those with whom I was in a fraternity or played basketball. It's as if I can feel the testosterone in the air. It's not a bad feeling; it's just different.

On the subject of athletes, once I asked my former college coach and now assistant coach for the L.A. Clippers, Armond Hill, about the problem that the NFL was having with players becoming increasingly violent off the field. What he said blew me away. He thought that the reason was fairly simple: football players actually "practice violence." That's what they do for a living, and they have been doing it for most of their adult lives. How can you turn that off? How can you go from practicing violence to practicing love and kindness? It's not so easy.

He added that he's been at awards banquets and other functions with lots of professional or ex-professional football players, and the energy they bring to the situation is palpable. It's as if they're on edge, ready to blow at any moment. Having been to some of those events, I knew exactly what he was talking about. That's an example of the kind of angry energy that is always best to avoid.

What does the concept of energy's being real mean for your daily life? To me, it's as simple as hanging out with people I feel good around, and choosing not to be with people who don't bring out the best in me.

If you run into an asshole in the morning, you ran into an asshole. If you run into assholes all day, you're the asshole.

—RAYLAN GIVENS, *JUSTIFIED*

The Power of Optimism

OPTIMISM CAN MAKE ALL THE difference to our emotional wellth. It can also make a difference in an outcome, especially in sports. In his book *Learned Optimism*, Dr. Martin Seligman finds a direct correlation between optimism and winning versus pessimism and losing. Even better, he explains how we can learn optimism through the ABCDE method. Earlier, psychologist Albert Ellis had developed the ABC model:

<u>A</u>dversity—Someone cuts you off in traffic.

<u>B</u>elief—You then think, "What a jerk!"

<u>C</u>onsequence—You scream at the driver, "Hey you jerk, don't cut me off!"

Seligman took the ABC model and added the D and the E:

<u>D</u>isputation—This is where you provide some counterevidence, such as, "Maybe the driver is in a rush because there's an emergency at home."

<u>E</u>nergization—This is where you take a moment to celebrate that you didn't flip out over getting cut off.

Seligman also points out the differences between optimists and pessimists:

The optimists and the pessimists. I have been studying them for the past twenty-five years. The defining characteristic of pessimists is that they tend to believe bad events will last a long time, will undermine everything they do, and are their own fault. The optimists, who are confronted with the same hard knocks of this world, think about misfortune in the opposite way. They tend to believe defeat is just a temporary setback, that its causes are confined to this one case. The optimists believe defeat is not their fault: circumstances, bad luck, or other people brought it about. Such people are unfazed by defeat. Confronted by a bad situation, they perceive it as a challenge and try harder.

So are you an optimist or a pessimist? The good news is that you can change your point of view and positively affect your emotional health.

Always Listen to Your Gut

ANOTHER ASPECT OF OPTIMIZING YOUR emotional wellth is knowing when to act according to your instincts. When you have a strong sense that something isn't right, or that you have to behave in a certain way, it's always good to go with your gut. I speak from experience.

It was a normal sunny Tuesday morning in September. I was sitting at my trading desk at Heartland, which was located at 50 Broad Street, a few blocks from the World Trade Center. The S&P futures (an indicator of whether the stock market was going to open up or down and also a signaler of breaking news) were fairly flat. Then all of a sudden, they took a nose-dive. Something was definitely going on.

My eyes were glued to CNBC as it reported that there had been an explosion at the World Trade Center. There was a lot of confusion as to what caused the explosion—reports ranged from a small plane crashing to possibly a bomb. Then there was another explosion in the second tower. After that, it became very clear that planes had flown into the towers.

Something was very wrong. I had the strongest and darkest feeling that I have ever experienced in my life. I needed to get the hell out of there, immediately. People on the floor were discussing what happened, trying to get hold of associates, friends, or loved ones that worked near there or in one of the towers. And people were just standing around, talking about it.

I called my mother from the landline and told her what had happened. I said that I was okay, but that I was leaving work immediately and was coming out to her home on Long Island. On the spur of the moment, I'd decided not to go back to my apartment in Chelsea. I looked out the window and saw small debris floating in the air. I shouted to my coworkers that I was leaving and that they should leave right away. I didn't even bother going to the elevators; I went straight for the stairs and ran down fifteen flights.

The debris on the street was getting worse. What I will never forget, and still don't understand to this day, was that I seemed to be the only person walking very fast *away* from the World Trade Center. People were walking around leisurely, and some were even walking toward the towers. They weren't running to help people, either; they were just standing around like deer in headlights.

I went to an ATM and withdrew as much money as I could, then got quarters from a deli, as cell phones were now jammed with the influx of calls. I ran toward the Williamsburg Bridge and hopped into a cab and gave the driver my mother's address. It was then that I heard on the radio that the first tower had collapsed. By the time I got home, the second tower had collapsed. When I walked in the door, I hugged my mother and grandmother—and broke down and cried.

This is an extreme case of having an instinct that literally sweeps you off your feet when there's danger. Fear can be so important to our survival. But whatever the definition, my 9/11 experience was a massive wave of gut feelings, and I've always been glad that I acted on them immediately.

I believe we all have little riptides when it comes to our gut feelings, good or bad. Whether it's as simple as choosing what to buy at the grocery store, or as complicated as hiring a key addition to your team at work, listening to these waves is the right way to go. The more you pay attention to them, the more you feel them, and the more powerful they become. Some can even feel like tsunamis. You can try to ignore your instincts, but you won't have much success. The wave or gut reaction is part of something much bigger than you are, and in the end, it will always win. If you try to go up against your intuition, you'll likely end up getting hurt. Some might just be little scrapes, but with monster waves, the consequences are much more serious.

Whenever I haven't listened to my gut, it's been disastrous.

From girlfriends to business partners to everyday decisions, whenever I've had the feeling that something wasn't right, it ended up not being right. And on the flip side, whenever things *did* feel right—whenever I had the feeling that this person, place, or thing was the right entity to be with or do—it ended up being perfect.

—— Grow Your Life Savings: Feel ——

COUNSELOR AND AUTHOR SHERYL PAUL has some interesting things to say about the word *should* and how it adversely affects our emotional well-being and our relationships.

I hear the following from my clients all the time:

I should attend that function tonight.

I should feel more excited to socialize.

I should feel happier over the holidays.

I should spend more time practicing mindfulness.

I should eat better foods.

As soon as I hear a *should* statement, I know that my client is suffering from an externally imposed expectation, and inevitably comparing her- or himself to a cultural ideal of good or right behavior.

Let's take the statement *I should feel more excited to socialize.* We carry a cultural idea that says that if you're socially cool or a good friend, you'll always want to see your friends. If you're an introvert, you may want to socialize with one or two friends, but spending time in large groups regularly will drain your energy. If you haven't embraced your personality type and temperament, your mind may go to: *There's something wrong with me* and then an anxious spiral can begin.

But you can see that the anxiety originates from the *should* statement, which, again, is an indicator that you're holding yourself to an external standard of right feeling or behavior. There are no right feelings in friendships; there is only what works for you.

Let's explore another *should* statement: *I should spend more time practicing mindfulness.* While mindfulness is proven to increase well-being, if you're practicing mindfulness because you *should* do it and not because you truly want to do it, you'll quickly find the practice dwindling away into a sea of self-created resentment as you resist what's good for you, because you feel controlled by your own externally imposed requirements for being a better person!

Since so many people grew up listening to a litany of rules, when the word *should* infiltrates your own running commentary, you will likely respond to yourself the same way you responded to well-meaning caregivers and authority figures: with resistance (since no one wants to feel controlled).

And yet another *should* statement: *I should attend that function tonight.* A few weeks ago a friend of mine was invited to a holiday function at her husband's company. She hadn't had a day off from work in weeks and she was exhausted, but she felt obligated to attend because she knew it was expected and her husband would feel disappointed if she declined. "I just want to go home and have a hot bath," she told me.

"So why don't you?" I asked. "That's clearly what you really want to do."

But her sense of should-derived guilt overrode her heart's desire, and she ended up attending the event, then picking a fight with her husband on the way home. Since she wasn't able to find a way to attend with true goodwill, I'm sure her husband would have preferred to deal with his own disappointment rather than spend the evening with a wife who didn't want to be there.

Can you imagine how much more lovingly she would have received her husband when he returned home had she spent the evening attending to her own needs?

Actions derived from *shoulds* are not truly loving to anyone. Since my friend attended the function because she was trying to be a good wife, she was betraying not only herself but also her partner. Now, this isn't to say that there aren't times when we need to assess the greater good and put our individual needs aside, but when we repeatedly ignore our inner *no* to please others, the results are ultimately disastrous.

To heal from the addiction to *should*, start to notice how often the word populates your self-talk, and then notice how you feel when you fall prey to believing the statement. When you hear the word *should*, ask: *What would be most loving to myself and others right now?* Then listen closely for the answer.

A QUICK DEPOSIT IN YOUR WELLTH ACCOUNT

- Social groups exert power over us, even as adults. Resist being a sheep in the herd and think for yourself.
- Consider the five people who influence you most. Are you receiving positive energy from them or the opposite?
- Instincts can be powerful indicators of what you should do. Never ignore your gut.
- Can you think of a past experience where you didn't listen to your gut? What happened?

CHAPTER 8

Love

IN THE PREVIOUS CHAPTER ON emotional health, we learned about the importance of accepting and loving oneself. You can't be happy if you're always down on yourself, giving in to that critical inner voice. But another powerful component of wellth is feeling loved by another person or persons. This doesn't only mean that you have to currently be in a love relationship with the opposite sex. In this chapter, I'll discuss both romantic and platonic connections and how these ingredients make up a large and delicious slice of the wellth pie.

Only if you find peace within yourself will you find true connection with others.

—THE ROSE PEDDLER, *BEFORE SUNRISE*

You are 100 percent responsible for your own happiness. No one thing or place—and especially no one person—can make you happy. Relationships can succeed only when each individual takes responsibility for their own expectations and doesn't expect their partner to fulfill them. When you depend on others to make you happy, it not only negatively affects your partner, but it places your identity and sense of self-worth in someone else's hands. It doesn't matter how loving, caring, and magical the hands are; your identity and self-worth shouldn't be there.

Let's say we have a couple named Dick and Jane. And let's say we're measuring happiness by ounces of water. Jane has a full sixteen-ounce cup of happiness, while Dick has only eight ounces. Collectively they have twenty-four ounces, but Jane is contributing two-thirds of their total happiness. And that's not good for either of them, as one person is depleted and making up for it by taking the other's surplus. It's okay in the short-term but unsustainable beyond that.

In my experience, being responsible for your own happiness is the essential building block of any relationship. But to be truly happy, you need to be your true self, as does your partner. You must love and support them in their journey, and they must do the same for you. This ability to express your true self is a building block of happiness and of any essential relationship.

It is appropriate for spiritual partners to remain together only as long as they grow together.
—GARY ZUKAV, *THE SEAT OF THE SOUL*

The first time I fell in love, it was magical. It was as if a whole new world had opened up. I was in love with being in love. It was new, it was exciting, and I was swept up in it. I was also twenty-three. (Yes, I do believe that age plays a role in whether relationships can go the distance.)

I was a senior in college with only a few weeks to go before I graduated (by a hair). The day before graduation I had to beg a teacher to change a D to a C. She changed the grade, and I squeaked by. To give you an idea of my priorities back then, I had even thrown out my desk to make room for a bar.

In college, I'd had no real romantic relationships—they were mostly flings, never evolving into anything real. Deep down I wanted something that transcended an awkward conversation (or lack thereof) the next morning, but it never happened. I think this lack of connection was partly due to the hookup culture in college and partly because I wasn't ready for anything more meaningful.

But this particular one-night stand turned into my first love and a relationship that lasted for three years. Over time, though, our relationship changed. We were still in love, but our interactions had become volatile. We fought more and more, and trust eroded, even though we still loved each other.

Then she decided to spend a semester abroad in Barcelona. It was something she had always wanted to do, and she was determined to go. Selfishly, I wanted her to stay. I wanted her to care so much about me—about *us*—that she wouldn't want to leave. I wanted someone who put me first, before any of her own goals or dreams. My heart was being broken for the first time, but not because she chose to go to Barcelona. It was because the person who I'd thought was my soul mate was not—or maybe she was a soul mate but not in the way I defined it at the time.

I visited her in Barcelona twice, and at the end of her semester she moved back to New York. But it wasn't the same, and we both knew it. She was distant and told me that although she still loved me, something had changed while she was abroad. I didn't want to hear her explanation, and I didn't understand her. I had always thought that love could conquer all. But now she was saying that love wasn't enough. Or maybe it was just the wrong kind of love.

She was right. We broke up, and I was a mess. My career was just taking off at the time; I had made over $280,000 in just one month's trading bonus, yet I was completely unhappy. I would have given all that money back to have our relationship return to the way it first was.

I no longer believed in the idea of soul mates, or love at first sight. But I was beginning to believe that a very few times in your life, if you were lucky, you might meet someone who was exactly right for you. Not because he was perfect, or because you were, but because your combined flaws were arranged in a way that allowed two separate beings to hinge together.

—LISA KLEYPAS, *BLUE-EYED DEVIL*

I self-medicated by turning to booze and women. The breakup, the fighting, the insecurities that had been boiling up inside me for the past few years had taken a toll. Breakups are hard no matter the circumstances, but this was particularly devastating to me. And the sudden accumulation of wealth was in such sharp contrast to having my personal life fall apart. I had lost myself in this relationship. Now I had to learn to be responsible for my own happiness and not assume that someone else would take care of that aspect of my life. But I'd lost all perspective.

They say that the best way to get over someone is to meet someone else, but I had no interest in that. After all the pain and heartache, my new vision of personal success was to have lots of money and lots of women and to not settle down until much later in life. At the time, the film *The Thomas Crown Affair* with Pierce Brosnan came out, and I remember thinking, "I want to be that guy!" He was beyond rich, and he wasn't interested in settling down until his late forties. Thomas Crown (minus the heists) was my new hero.

I went out to all the best restaurants and bars in New York. I partied my brains out, and I went home with a different woman almost every weekend. I was drinking and carousing to forget about my heartache.

My self-esteem had been completely beaten down, but sleeping around made me feel a little better about myself. The fact that women were attracted to me, wanted to be with me, boosted my ego. Someone had rejected me, and it hurt. Now I could go out every weekend and find someone attractive who'd accept me. This strategy helped somewhat, but not for long. The thing about one-night stands is that they do make you feel better about yourself for a brief moment, but they get very old very fast. I still longed for something real, someone to love, someone to hold and share a life with. But I wasn't ready for her yet.

My next serious relationship was with someone I met on

a flight. The relationship was brief—only four months—but I fell hard and I fell fast. When we split up, once again I was heartbroken. I cried and almost cursed God, asking, "Why would you do this to me again? I didn't want this, and you made this happen again! Why?"

One thing that became an issue between us was the fact that I had slept around so much in the past. After we broke up, I realized that promiscuity wasn't the answer. Before I met her, I had planned to live the bachelor life, being with one woman after another. Now I went in a completely different direction, vowing that the next woman I slept with would be the person I married. This was an extreme and not the answer, but I decided that I'd had my fill of hookups and heartbreak and needed to focus only on myself for the time being.

No matter what happens around you, don't take it personally. . . . Nothing other people do is because of you. It is because of themselves.

—DON MIGUEL RUIZ, *THE FOUR AGREEMENTS*

Three Types of Soul Mates

I BELIEVE THAT THERE ARE three different types of soul mates. The first is the one that you aren't meant to be with forever but that delivers powerful lessons. These soul mates tend to be the most influential teachers in our lives. They're the ones that provide the heartache, the ones that don't work out and aren't meant to work out. The second type is the one that allows you to be your true self and who stays with you forever. The third type is a platonic friend with whom you are always connected to and feel you can share your innermost thoughts and emotions.

In my first serious relationship, I learned that a great six months, or a great year, or a great few years—and all the love and affection in the world—don't always make for a lasting relationship. Love isn't always enough. You can love someone, and they can love you, but it doesn't mean you're meant to be together. Your partner should make you better, and your partner should make you whole. In fact, I think they should make you more than whole and especially not less. One plus one should not equal one point five or two; it should equal three.

My second relationship helped me to heal after being hurt so badly. Although she wasn't my forever soul mate, she helped me get my act together. Boy, was I off track when I met her. I was ready to keep on making lots of money by trading, and I was trading sexual partners as well. I needed a huge course correction, and that's precisely what I got.

The next type of soul mate is the one in which one plus one equals three. He or she is the one that makes you better, the one that allows you to be your true self and to feel comfortable in a way you probably felt only when you were a small child. This soul mate lets you be you and *helps* you be your most authentic self. They're the icing on the cake. A cake by itself can be pretty delicious, but when you get that yummy icing on top, it's unforgettable. You meet each other precisely when you're both ready, not a moment before or a moment after. The expression "timing is everything" is especially true with this kind of soul mate.

I've found this to be true over and over in life, especially with regard to relationships. Just when you're about ready to give up—when you've had enough of dating, enough of the games, enough of the heartbreak, not a moment too early and not a moment too late—at that very time, when you're truly ready and open to anything, the right person comes into your life.

The course of true love never did run smooth.

—WILLIAM SHAKESPEARE, *A MIDSUMMER NIGHT'S DREAM*

Colleen and I met on a blind date on November 9, 2007. At the time, I was living in New York and Chicago, but I was in San Francisco for a week on business. Once again timing was everything. The person who set us up was a mutual friend who had known both of us for a while but for some reason hadn't introduced us until then. The blind date was at a cheesy wine bar in the Marina section of San Francisco, and it lasted for six hours.

Looking back, it was not our scene, so it's kind of funny we first met at a place that neither of us would ever go to. I'll never forget seeing her for the first time. My friend and I were having a glass of wine, and she came up from the side. I saw her through a different type of lens of beautiful, which I still have trouble describing. We talked about everything from restaurants to art to doughnuts. The conversation flowed effortlessly. She was beautiful, smart, kind, and funny. And she loved old people! Anyone whose heart melts when they come across a senior citizen has a special place in my heart. We closed the date by getting chocolate doughnuts. We got a cab, and I dropped her off outside her apartment. There was no kiss, and I didn't even ask for her number.

But something had changed that night. When she was about to step out of the taxi, I was sure I'd see her again. I had this strange inner knowing that I'd never felt before. The next day I tracked down her number from our mutual friend, and then we spent hours talking on the phone. (Here again I was breaking rules, like "not calling a girl the day after a first date." Not only was it the first date, it was the morning after—before noon!)

On our second date a week later, we went to a cute French bistro in Russian Hill. Beforehand Colleen had had to fly to New York for a few days for work. She got the last seat on a flight back to San Francisco and barely made it in time for our date before I had to leave. You frequent fliers out there will appreciate the miracle of Colleen getting on a flight ahead of coworkers with superior status. It really was a miracle that she caught that flight. If she hadn't, we wouldn't have had our second date because I was heading back to New York the next day. And if we'd never had that second date, then I wouldn't have kissed her. I wouldn't have had that moment where I knew (from just one kiss and nothing more) that I had met the woman I would marry—my soul mate, the forever kind. But these are the kinds of soul mates that you can't just write a chapter about. They're the ones you write books about.

One of the things that sealed the deal for me was our continuous conversation that flowed for hours without a moment of boredom. You find yourself sharing things you don't typically share and being interested in things you normally wouldn't be. You go from glancing around to see who else is nearby to fixating on the person across from you. You feel a sense of urgency to share almost everything that is going on in your life—not only the good but also the bad.

And it wasn't about how quickly Colleen would sleep with me. Instead, it was about how quickly I could win her heart. As I said, after our second date, we had our first kiss (and nothing more!), and at that point I knew she was the woman I would marry. A few months later we were already discussing marriage. I never had a doubt or last-minute cold feet along the way. I proposed to her one year later, and we got married sixteen months after we first met.

Loving someone and having them love you back is the most precious thing in the world.

—NICHOLAS SPARKS, *THE RESCUE*

Love, Defined

WHAT DOES *LOVE* MEAN? LOVE goes beyond infatuation. Sure, you have to be attracted to your partner, but attraction will last only so long. It must go deeper. It must be stronger. You must love someone for who they are, not for who you want them to be. True love is altruistic; it means putting another person's needs before your own. It means you will stick with that person even if they become ill or depressed or their appearance changes. It means that as you age, you will grow together and not resist or resent the other person's growth. And together you bring out the best in each other.

To sum up, I believe we have two kinds of romantic soul mates. The first are the ones who aren't meant to last, the ones who help get you from point A to B and make sure you learn the lessons that you need to learn. The second kind of soul mate is the one who allows you to be your true self, the one who stays with you forever. When you're with the person you're meant to be with, they don't bring out your insecurities. They actually make them go away. They bring out the best in you, not the worst. You and your partner are both happy with your true selves, and together you make each other even happier. In this ideal scenario, one plus one equals three.

The third kind of soul mate is the nonromantic kind. This type is the most similar to the first kind, except that there's no romance and definitely no sex! We all have these good friends; in fact, most of us have experienced many of them in our lifetimes. They're the people who you haven't seen or spoken to in weeks, months, or years—but whenever you do see or speak to each other, you pick up wherever you left off, as if neither of you had missed a beat. They're also the ones who you connect with very deeply and frequently for a period in your life. Sometimes the two of you grow apart, or someone moves away or has a life event that distances you. Other times you'll remain lifelong close friends, even if you see each other only once or twice a year.

These types of soul mates are plentiful in our lives. I've had many, ranging from the partners in crime who were always up for an adventure to John Derderian, with whom I've been friends since childhood, and Austin Milliken, who was attached to my hip in college—or should I say attached to my barstool. These are just a few of the long list of non-romantic soul mates I've had over the years. I've had soul mates who were in and out of my life for just a few weeks, who were the friends I needed to keep me on track while I wavered from my path. There are the ones with whom I shared a unique experience, a kinship over jobs, moves, or loss.

And then there are the people who are in your life for a blink of an eye (or a godwink, as it were), who say or do exactly what you need at that moment, then disappear forever. It can take the form of a compliment in an elevator from a complete stranger. Or an off-hand comment from a grocery store cashier that encourages you to stay on your healthy diet. You know who these people are in your life, although perhaps you haven't considered them as soul mates. But they have given your soul something it needs. These nonromantic fellow humans who give gentle boosts along your journey are with us every step of the way.

One of the things I'd learned . . . was how to take a compliment. Just say, "Thank you." It's the only response a confident person can make.

—NEIL STRAUSS, *THE GAME*

Soul mate or no soul mate, relationships are hard work. It takes lots of effort to make even the best relationship last through life's twist and turns. Yes, your soul mate(s) is or are out there, but what do you do when life happens? Is there one "forever" romantic soul mate for a person, or are there multiple soul mates waiting for you? For example, if you don't meet your romantic soul mate in your twenties, is another one waiting for you in your thirties? I think that this is so.

Communication Is Key

IT'S NOT ONLY ADVERSITY, SUCH as money or health issues, that can strain and sometimes break what was once a strong bond. It's the little things that slowly erode a relationship over time and can change a beautiful skyscraper with a strong foundation into a building filled with cracks that is likely to crumble. It's often the little things that add up over time that can derail what was once a healthy, great relationship.

There are little things that matter and little things that don't. It drives me nuts when Colleen doesn't put all the dishes in the dishwasher, and it drives her nuts when I don't clean the toilet. But in the whole scheme of things, both aren't that important. Little things that do matter are all about communication, specifically a breakdown or lack of understanding around your partner's communication patterns and vice versa.

For example, when Colleen is stressed, she turns to self-care mode, going for a facial, acupuncture, or doing yoga. I used to try to force her to talk about what was stressing her out and provide an optimistic silver lining to whatever was ailing her, but that wasn't what she wanted. All she wanted was for me to listen and not provide any recommendations or spin. She wanted me to let her take care of herself in her own way. I'm the opposite; when I'm stressed, I want to talk about it. I'm almost incapable of holding it in. Over time we have learned each other's communication patterns and how to accommodate them.

Soul Mates Are Crucial

WHEREVER YOU'RE IN YOUR JOURNEY toward finding a "forever" type of partner, keep in mind that there are three types of soul mates. Even if you sense that the person you're currently involved with won't be with you forever, realize that you're learning things from this person that will help you on your way to eventually finding that one great relationship. And our platonic soul mates raise our spirits when we're down, make the great times even better, and help us get through the bad times.

—— Grow Your Life Savings: Love ——

ONE OF MY FAVORITE EXPERTS on the topic of relationships is my friend Dr. Sue Johnson. Here is her advice about some pitfalls to avoid with romantic soul mates as well as tips to create an incredible romantic relationship:

FIVE WAYS TO RUIN A PERFECTLY GOOD RELATIONSHIP

Theories that concentrate on bad behavior and lack of communication skills focus on the *symptoms* of a couple's distress rather than the root cause: the overwhelming fear of being emotionally abandoned, set adrift in the sea of life without a safe harbor.

Discord is almost always an unconscious protest against floating loose and an attempt to call, and even force, a partner back into emotional connection. Here are some of the signs of discord:

1. **The slow erosion.** When emotional starvation becomes the norm, and negative patterns of outraged criticism and defensiveness take over, our perspective changes. Our lover begins to feel like an enemy; our most familiar friend turns into a stranger. Trust dies, and grief begins in earnest.

2. **Poisonous criticism.** We never like to hear that there is something wrong with us, or that something needs changing, especially if this message is coming from a loved one. Criticism from loved ones sets off the deep-seated fear that we will be rejected and abandoned.

3. **Toxic stonewalling.** We all use withdrawal at times when we are hurt or offended, or simply worried about saying the wrong thing. It's like a pause in the duet with our partner; it can allow us to gather our thoughts, and find our balance. But withdrawal is toxic when it becomes the habitual response to a partner's perceived blaming. When we stonewall, we cut off our emotions;

we freeze and retreat into numbness. But when one dancer completely leaves the floor, the dance is no more.

4. **Dead end.** As the cycle of hostile criticism and stonewalling occurs more often, it becomes ingrained and starts to define the relationship. These episodes are so destructive that any positive behaviors are discounted. And as a couple's behavior narrows, so do the partners' views of each other. They shrink in each other's eyes: she's a carping bitch; he's a withholding boor. Both partners become hypervigilant for any hint of slurs and slights. They cannot give each other the benefit of the doubt, even for a moment.

5. **The sudden snap.** An affair can cripple a relationship, but other events may be just as damaging because they contradict our expectations that loved ones will be our shelter at moments of distress. If we do not understand the incredible power of attachment, we can inadvertently hurt our partner by not understanding what kind of response is required. All such disastrous events are marked by moments of intense need and vulnerability, when a loved one is called upon to provide responsive care and does not come through. In these incidents, the answer to the key attachment questions—"Are you there for me when I need you?" and "Will you put me first?"—is a resounding no.

These failures of empathy and responsiveness create wounds that cannot be put aside. Most people recognize these wounds on a gut level when they are describing them, and many do not believe that they can be healed. But indeed they can, even when they occur in relationships that are already faltering.

HOW TO HAVE THE BEST RELATIONSHIP ——— OF YOUR LIFE

You can create a fulfilling, safe-haven relationship, restoring the romantic love bond, beginning now.

Abandon the out-of-date idea that love is something that just happens to you. All the new science tells us that romantic love is no longer a mystery. It makes perfect sense. You can learn its laws. You have more control over this riot of emotion than you think! And what you understand, you can shape. The first step is to decide to learn about love and the new science of bonding.

Every day, try openly reaching out to someone and asking for their attention or affection. Accept that love is an ancient, wired-in survival code. You are happier, healthier, and stronger; you deal with stress better; and you live longer when you nurture your bonds with your loved ones. It is okay to need them; they are your greatest resource. We are not designed for self-sufficiency. The strongest among us accept this need for connection.

The next time you feel uncertain or worried or anxious, try just mentioning it to your partner; or notice their emotional signals and reach for their hand. The bonds of love offer us a safe haven where we can take shelter and regain our emotional balance. The latest study in our lab shows that just holding your loved one's hand can calm your brain and shut down fear.

See if you can notice times when you find openness hard and you become defensive or distant or shut down. We know that emotional openness and responsiveness are the ground on which solid, lasting bonds stand. See if you can take the initiative and share with your partner, helping him or her understand what makes it hard to be open for you.

Reflect on how you and your partner usually interact. Can each of you reach out for the other? What do you do when your partner gets upset or does not respond to you? Do you push for contact or move away? Tell your partner one thing they could do to help you reach for them rather than moving away from them.

Try to talk with your partner about how you affect each other. Both of you offer safety or danger cues that the brain takes as serious survival information; we are all vulnerable when alone. When do you arouse real joy or contentment with your partner? When do you spark distress—a sense of being rejected or alone? Our brains code this kind of hurt in the same place and in the same way as physical pain.

When you get into a fight, take a deep breath and try to see the fight as if you were a fly on the ceiling. Often underneath the discussion of problematic issues, someone is asking for more emotional connection. See if you can get curious and pinpoint the dance; maybe it's on the floor where one pushes for contact, but the other hears criticism and steps back. See how it leaves you both feeling alone and a little scared. Talk about that.

Invite your partner into more closeness once a day by playing a simple empathy game. Each person thinks of an event in their day. Then you take turns at reading each other's face and trying to pinpoint whether you see one of the six basic emotions: joy, surprise, sadness, anger, shame/embarrassment, or some kind of fear. See if your guess is right.

Take a quiet moment and see if you can each share with each other what you need most. Keep it simple and concrete. Do you need comfort, reassurance, support, and empathy, a clear message of how important you are to him or her? If it's too hard to share this, share how hard it is to open up and ask.

Be mindful of the fact that emotional injuries derail relationships. You can inflict great pain on your partner simply because you matter so much—you are the one he or she depends on. At a close moment, ask your lover if there are injuries that are unhealed, perhaps times when you missed their cues for support. Try to help them with this hurt. Often just telling them that you can feel how they hurt and want to help works wonders.

Honor your connection. Create small rituals to recognize your bond. Maybe it's a special kind of kiss when you leave in the morning, or a special ten-minute bonding time when you first come home. This is sacred time. No business agendas, problem solving, or distractions in the form of small electronic screens are allowed.

A QUICK DEPOSIT IN YOUR WELLTH ACCOUNT

- There are two types of romantic soul mates: those who temporarily help us along our life's journeys and who teach us important lessons; and our "forever" soul mate, who stays the course.
- All the love and affection in the world don't always make for a lasting relationship. A romantic soul mate should make you better than you are, so that one plus one equals three.
- The third type of soul mate is not romantic but is a friend with whom we have a deep connection. Even if we lose touch with this person, if we see them again, we can pick up with them right where we left off.
- All three kinds of soul mates are crucial in our journey toward a fulfilling life.

CHAPTER 9

Heal

SINCE PHYSICAL HEALTH IS OBVIOUSLY important to wellth, we have to become adept at healing that which goes wrong in our bodies. Sometimes we can heal ourselves through self-care such as yoga, rest, and nutrition, but other times we have to rely on the help of experts.

> *When health is absent, wisdom cannot reveal itself, art cannot manifest, strength cannot fight, wealth becomes useless, and intelligence cannot be applied.*
>
> —HEROPHILUS

In the fall of 2012, I began to feel very fatigued and anxious. At first, I thought my ennui was stress-related, as Hurricane Sandy had just hit New York City. In a lot of ways, the disaster brought back the feelings of the days following 9/11. The city was on lockdown, and the atmosphere was ominous.

I decided to combat the stress by getting back to my yoga practice, meditating more, and upping my consumption of green juice. But none of that worked. I still felt terrible, and I was constantly tired. I'd take a midday two-hour nap after a full night's sleep. I really couldn't figure it out. I thought I might need a vacation, so Colleen and I flew down to Miami for a few days to relax on the beach and lie low. But that didn't relieve my symptoms, either.

I finally saw my friend Dr. Frank Lipman, who thought that I might have a parasite or "bug," as he called it. I was so happy he knew what was wrong, because I was starting to worry that there were no answers for why I felt so awful. He suggested that I see Dr. Kevin Cahill, a tropical medicine doctor on the Upper East Side, who specialized in such diagnoses.

Frank picked up the phone, called Cahill's office, and insisted that they make room to see me the next morning. They agreed, and then Frank told me that I was going to be okay. A great doctor knows that those words, "You're going to be okay," go a long way toward making someone feel much better.

In my case, they did. As I walked out of Frank's office, he added, "Cahill is a character." I nodded and was on my way, excited that I would finally get some answers.

The next day I showed up at Dr. Cahill's Fifth Avenue ground-floor office in time for my eight a.m. appointment. He asked me if I had been to any third-world countries lately, and I said I had not. He mentioned that overseas travel can lead to a higher incidence of parasites, but he also said that they're more prevalent here in the United States than we know or care to admit. "It's always the same story," he added. "There's a new sous chef in a restaurant who forgets to wash his hands." I got the picture, but it wasn't an image I wanted to focus on.

Dr. Cahill took a sample and said he would get back to me

with a full diagnosis in the morning. I said okay. After almost a month of feeling completely awful, I was going to get some answers.

The next morning I called his office to check on my test results. Sure enough, I had a parasite called amebiasis (also known as *Entamoeba histolytica*). I was told to take antibiotics and an antifungal medication that was usually given to women for yeast infections. Since I'm a bit skeptical of medication, especially antibiotics, I called Frank and told him about the diagnosis. Before I even got to my question about the drugs, he said, "You need to take the antibiotics."

Frank said I'd soon start to feel better. I should supplement the pills with herbs and probiotics, he added, in an effort to keep the parasites from coming back and to restore my gut health. Apparently parasites are tough to get rid of, as they tend to move around the gut and the microbiome. If you're not familiar with the term *microbiome*, you should be, as it's the future of medicine and truly a blend of Eastern and Western thought.

Living in our guts are billions of microbes and bacteria that are collectively called the microbiome. Scientists are coming to believe that it is literally the key to our health. We are made up of more than 100 trillion bacteria, both good and bad. Our bodies are 90 percent microbes, and the microbiome influences everything health-related. And guess what influences the microbiome? Our diet and the state of our guts.

An antibiotic kills not only the bad bacteria but also the good bacteria. This is why you should always take a probiotic for three to six months after taking antibiotics. But there's still a lot we don't know—for example, how exactly the microbiome interacts with other systems in the body to influence digestion and metabolism. Companies such as Ubiome sell microbiome kits in which you can send saliva and stool samples that will provide information on your microbial makeup. The science isn't perfect yet, however, so I'm not sure how useful this test is to date.

I took the pills for two weeks and supplemented with herbs and probiotics. Western medicine would have nuked my gut in an effort to kill the bad guys, and Eastern medicine would have nourished and restored my gut back to health. For the first time, I realized how powerful the blend of Eastern and Western medicine could be.

I started to think more about this blending and times when I'd experienced it before. My back pain came to mind. Through an MRI (Western), I learned that I had two extruded disks in my lower back. However, it was through yoga (Eastern) that I healed my back pain. Since a mix of the two philosophies had cured my back, I was hopeful that the combined wisdom would solve my gut problem.

The doctor of the future will no longer treat the human frame with drugs, but rather will cure and prevent disease with nutrition.

—THOMAS EDISON

I kept taking the herbs, and I also decided to purify my diet. I began juicing heavily. Many people in the wellness community swore by the health benefits of colon hydrotherapy, so I decided to give it a try, too.

A few weeks into juicing and colon hydrotherapy, I was still feeling up and down. I was getting fatigued again, and I was becoming frustrated. I thought I had kicked this thing, and yet I still wasn't feeling 100 percent. I went back to see Frank, and he suggested I take a food sensitivity blood test, which could screen for sensitivities to everything from foods to herbs to cosmetics and more. A week later Frank told me that I was allergic to celery and also had strong sensitivities to Brazil nuts, fertilizer, and licorice. This explained a lot; here I was chugging green juice that was full of celery in an effort to cleanse my system. Most green juices use celery as filler, and I was drinking it by the gallon. No wonder I felt like crap! As a child, I absolutely hated the odor of fertilizer, as well as the scent of licorice. Perhaps my allergies were the reason I loathed those smells?

This blood test was another win for Western medicine. Over the next two years, overcoming the parasite would remain an uphill battle as it returned twice, which led to two more rounds of antibiotics and herbs. Finally I've gone a year without any symptoms. I hope I've really kicked it this time.

I learned a lot through this experience. For starters, you don't have to go to a third-world country to get one of these bugs. You can pick one up at your local salad bar or in your favorite sushi restaurant. I'm convinced that millions of people have parasites but have no idea that they do. Parasites are hard to diagnose, and very few doctors properly test for them.

In addition, symptoms of parasites can run the gamut, and most doctors tend to write you off with a prescription for antacid or something stronger. You feel generally under the weather, and in some cases you can experience sensations that make absolutely no sense medically. I felt a tingling in my legs and groin, areas that no one would associate with the gut. When I had the tingling in my legs, I went to see a neurologist. He found nothing wrong and looked at me as if I were crazy when I told him that I had a parasite and asked if there was any connection.

But here's the thing: everything, and I mean *everything*, is gut-related and is interconnected. This is where the microbiome and the blend of East and West really come into play. I believe that this combination of principles is the absolute future of medicine.

There are more than one billion bacteria in each drop of fluid in your colon, an environment we call the microbiome. It's a mixture so distinctive from person to person that your individual constellation of bacteria is a more specific identifier than your own DNA.

—DR. ROBYNNE CHUTKAN, *GUTBLISS*

My friend Dr. Terry Wahls has basically cured her debilitating multiple sclerosis through diet and healing her gut. She went from being in a wheelchair to running again in just a few years, merely through diet and lifestyle changes. Terry essentially embraced the Paleo diet, cutting out grains and legumes. She ate greens, sulfur-rich vegetables, deeply colored vegetables, berries, grass-fed meat, wild fish, and seaweed. Then there's my friend, celebrity chef Seamus Mullen (another patient of Frank's), who went from having such painful severe rheumatoid arthritis that he could barely walk, to biking hundreds of miles. Seamus embraced a diet similar to Terry's. Both of them have helped themselves through healing their guts.

Eastern Versus Western Medicine

I'M A HUGE FAN OF Eastern medicine—acupuncture, shiatsu, reiki, cupping, herbs—you name it, I've done it. But do you know what? Eastern medicine isn't perfect. And I think we'd all agree that Western medicine has room for improvement, too. Western medicine is fantastic when it comes to diagnostics and critical care. Eastern healing is incredible when dealing with symptoms and diving deeper into root causes. If you believe that we are spiritual beings having human experiences, then you must also look at what's going on in your life spiritually. Depression, stress, and sadness may be contributing to the ailment you're experiencing.

We're at a particularly exciting and interesting time in regard to the meeting of Eastern and Western thinking. A number of doctors, like my friends Dr. Frank Lipman, Dr. Mark Hyman, and Dr. Robin Berzin, now practice this blend of "functional medicine." If you step into their offices, they'll treat you—and not your symptoms. They'll actually listen to you as you describe your symptoms, your diet, your stress levels, and so on. These guys go way beyond the run-of-the-mill tests at your standard check-up, such as blood pressure and cholesterol. Depending on what's going on, they'll probably run more sophisticated tests that most docs don't run, such as tests for food sensitivities or exposure to heavy metals.

And here's the kicker: once they have the results, they might prescribe medication, but they're probably more likely to prescribe dietary changes. You may be told to eat more greens and cut out sugar and gluten and perhaps to practice meditation to alleviate the stress that's been giving you that monkey mind—the constant chatter in your head about to-do lists and errands, or the what-can-go-wrong scenarios that play over and over. This is the stuff that seems to never allow you to just simply be and enjoy the moment.

Leveraging the power of Western diagnostics with Eastern methods is exciting. Not only does it minimize our pill culture, which treats only symptoms, it also empowers people to make food and lifestyle choices that actually treat root causes.

If I were to predict the future of medicine, I'd say that it will involve a personalized dietary prescription that caters to each individual's unique bacterial makeup. And for now? As Dr. Robynne Chutkan says, "Live dirty, eat clean."

Alternative Treatments to Consider

MY FRIEND DR. JOEL KAHN lectures widely on the cardiac benefits of plant-based nutrition and mind-body practices. He has this to say about the benefits of alternative treatments:

After twenty-five years of treating heart disease, I am familiar with the usual menu of pills, stents, and heart surgery. In my opinion, that narrow menu is limiting, as there are a number of healing therapies for the heart that have scientific support and that I have seen work. Massage, acupuncture and hands on healing like Reiki are worthy of mention towards a holistic approach to heart health.

Massage therapy. Is there any reason to believe a relaxing massage can be therapeutic for the heart? Indeed there is. For example, in 2008 researchers studied 263 volunteers who had a massage for 45 to 60 minutes. Their average blood pressure fell by 10 mm Hg, and their heart rate fell by ten beats per minute after one treatment. That's about as much as you might get from prescribing a new blood pressure medication for life! And other studies have backed up these findings. There is also a drop in markers of inflammation, which is intriguing as it suggests massage therapy may have a body-wide healing effect. Recent studies of massage therapy after both cardiac bypass surgery and stent placement have identified reduced anxiety and a smoother recovery with massage.

Acupuncture. Patients taught me the power of traditional Chinese medicine and acupuncture for heart conditions, and I now use it for four heart conditions and one behavior that leads to heart disease: smoking.

- **Angina** is a choking, squeezing, or pressurelike feeling in the chest brought on by activity and quickly relieved by rest or a nitro tablet. It usually results from a large heart artery that is severely blocked, but many patients have apparently normal arteries on angiography, and disease of small arteries is also suspected. Perhaps by reducing the action of the sympathetic nervous system to the heart muscle (the fight-or-flight system), selected patients with angina respond to acupuncture with less symptoms and better ability to walk long distances.

Congestive heart failure is a potentially serious condition that can result from a heart weakened by a heart attack or viral damage but is often seen with strong hearts that relax inadequately. Improvements in the ability to walk longer distances without shortness of breath after acupuncture therapy have been shown in research studies.

Arrhythmia is an irregularity of the heartbeat. The heart is an energy organ, and every beat is controlled by a wave of electricity and recovery. Acupuncture has been shown to affect the beat to improve the heart rate variability, a marker of better health.

Hypertension or high blood pressure can result from overdrive of the sympathetic nervous system. The rise in blood pressure can damage kidneys, arteries, eyes, and the brain. I have seen individual patients benefit from a lowering in blood pressure with a consistent practice of acupuncture, and the American College of Cardiology considers it a promising alternative therapy.

Smoking cessation is imperative, as smoking is still the number-one root cause of deaths due to heart disease and cancer. Acupuncture is one of the modalities that may help the nicotine-addicted patient to successfully quit this habit. More than three thousand patients have been studied in randomized trials of the role of acupuncture to quit smoking, and most favor a positive effect.

Therapeutic touch. Healing therapies utilizing touch or close physical proximity such as Reiki have been shown to have beneficial cardiac effects. These include fewer irregular heartbeats, regulated vitals signs, and decreased anxiety. Some fascinating facts about the heart may partially explain this benefit:

- The heart emits an electrical field 60 times greater in amplitude than the activity in the brain, and an electromagnetic field 5,000 times stronger than that of the brain. The electromagnetic field of the heart is incredibly strong. It can be measured anywhere on the body (using an EKG with electrodes on the ankles and wrists) and even several feet outside the body as well.
- Activity in one person's heart can be measured in the brain waves of another person. The electromagnetic field of two individuals (human, or pet and human), touching or within a few feet of each other, can interact so that energy activity in the heart of one individual is measured in the brain waves of the other. The act of touch for healing therapies may be due to this method of communication.
- The electrical activity of the heart and the brain can be guided into a synchronous electrical rhythm that can easily be measured and displayed by simply focusing on positive and loving emotions emanating from the heart. This state of organ "coherence" is associated with improved higher-level functioning, lower blood-pressure and cortisol levels, and improved immune system function.

It may be premature to consider massage therapy, acupuncture, and therapeutic touch to be on par with the science behind traditional medical care. However, given that tens of millions of people in the United States alone are at risk for heart disease, alternative approaches to the health of the heart and its nervous system are needed. For those who are so inclined, these therapies can join yoga, meditation, and Tai Chi as complementary approaches to maintaining optimal vascular health.

To keep the body in good health is a duty; otherwise we shall not be able to keep our mind strong and clear.

—BUDDHA

Don't Let Doctors Dictate Your Destiny

EVEN THOUGH WE NEED PHYSICIANS to help us heal, even the experts can be wrong at times. Always choose your doctor carefully, checking out his or her credentials and asking for references. The wrong diagnosis can be extremely damaging to you both physically and emotionally.

When I was three years old, my mother took me for a routine visit to the pediatrician. After the doctor examined me by giving a test of hand-eye coordination, she pulled my mother aside to tell her that I was brain-damaged and that it would be a miracle if I ever lived a normal life. Obviously, hearing this, my mother was extremely upset. She called my father, who simply said, "We'll be okay."

Then my mother went into I'll-do-whatever-I-can-so-that-my-son-has-a-normal-life mode. The next day when she dropped me off at preschool, she told my teachers about my potential special needs. My teachers expressed their doubts and volunteered to have a specialist come into the class and observe me. After observing me, the learning specialist determined that I was fine; that doctor had terrified my mother for no reason. My mother was so elated that I was okay that she didn't do anything except find me a new pediatrician. Not only was I not mentally disabled but I went on to graduate from an Ivy League college.

About a year after the pediatrician visit, another doctor told my mother that I was so knock-kneed, I'd never be able to play sports. He said I needed braces for my legs or even corrective surgery. However, my knees straightened out by themselves over the next few months after I got lifts in my shoes, and I went on to be a great athlete and a starter on a Division 1 basketball team.

Fast-forward to my twenties, when a doctor told me that I had herpes. (I didn't share this with my mother!) The diagnosis was unnerving, and when I was retested a few months later, it turned out that I *didn't* have it; the first test had been a false positive. Ironically, the same thing happened to Colleen before I met her. A false positive herpes test was one of the things we initially bonded over.

In my mid-thirties, two different surgeons told me I needed back surgery—and that it was nonnegotiable. You know how that story ends. I never got surgery and instead healed my back with yoga. Today I'm totally fine. The moral of this story? Doctors can be wrong. Trust your gut, and go after the right answers for you.

You could say that I have a history of doctors scaring the crap out of me. Don't get me wrong—I know that doctors save lives. But don't let doctors dictate your destiny—only you control your destiny. Never forget that.

Grow Your Life Savings: Heal

DR. AMY SHAH'S GOAL IS to help us combine Eastern, Western, and Internet medicine to achieve a life and body with which we're satisfied. Here is her advice about being the CEO of your own body:

I love traditional M.D.'s—they're my best friends, family, and trusted colleagues. They save lives and perform medical feats beyond imagination. But even though many doctors are smart, well-intentioned, and caring, many are not trained to optimize health, which is a completely different skill than performing life-saving surgery or individualizing chemotherapy.

The good news is that there are many professionals (including some forward-thinking M.D.'s) who can guide you to your healthiest self. But until you find that person, I urge you to become the CEO of your body and try some (or all) of the dozen ideas that follow.

Get extended blood testing. Your doctor may order some of these tests, but many are add-ons. You may get some push-back if your doctor is a minimalist, but the tests are worth pursuing even if you have to go to an outside lab like Wellnessfx, CanaryClub.org, DirectLabs, or AnyLabTestNow.

You'll want to order a complete blood count, which will give you information about your blood and can help pinpoint issues with fatigue and infection. It's also a good idea to order a complete thyroid panel and a complete lipid panel. Getting this data will give you a more complete assessment of your health and help you identify areas for improvement.

Get enough sleep. If there's one thing I could wish on every single one of you, it would be adequate sleep. Unfortunately, it's not always easy to prioritize our z's, let alone figure out how many hours we need for optimal health. Here's the easy way: just sleep for three to five days without an alarm to find out how much sleep you need to feel rested. For most of us, this is somewhere between seven and nine hours.

Manage your stress. Too much stress disrupts your hormones and your sleep and makes you gain weight. Worse, it can lead to long-term chronic inflammation and disease. (A classic example is the Wall Street executive who dies prematurely of a heart attack.) That's why meditation, yoga, or some kind of mindfulness practice every day is essential.

Need some extra help? Try taking Vitamin C (start with 1 g three times a day), fish oil (1–4 g a day), phosphatidylserine (400–800 mg a day), ashwagandha (300 mg twice a day), or rhodiola (200 mg twice a day). Use just one of these supplements at a time. Add another one only after using the first for a few weeks. We want to reset your system by getting to the root of the issue—not rely on supplements for an extended period of time.

Track your movement. Whether you use a pedometer, FitBit, FuelBand, or pencil and paper, tracking your movement during the day is important. Aim for 10,000 to 15,000 steps (about five miles) daily.

Check your resting pulse. Check your pulse when you wake up, before you even get out of bed. An ideal resting pulse is 60 beats per minute or below. (Athletes are routinely in the fifties.)

Fix your gut. As you know, the gut holds much of the bacteria in our bodies, and now we know that our immune system, brain, and hormones are intimately connected to it. This microbiome includes tens of trillions of bacteria that live on and in our bodies. Bloating, constipation, or frequent stomach pain is a good indicator that the gut may have some imbalances. An imbalanced gut can lead to food sensitivities, mood disorders, autoimmune problems, and other larger problems. In order to fix your gut, you have to determine your food intolerances (see below), get more sleep, and decrease your stress (see above). Another huge factor is to avoid antibiotics (unless you absolutely need them), as well as antibacterial soaps and products, and eat probiotic foods (natural sauerkraut, pickles, and kombucha). We are just now learning the immense power that fixing your gut can hold for your health.

Live creatively and with purpose. What do you do to unwind? This is an area many of us neglect. Some ideas to explore: volunteering, writing, painting, drawing, or cooking. Why? Getting in the zone with an enjoyable activity lowers stress hormones, increases happiness, and gives you something to look forward to every day. As a start, aim to have fun fifteen to thirty minutes every day.

Understand the truth about processed foods. Whether you decide to go Paleo or vegan or follow a Mediterranean diet, all these diets have one amazing thing in common: they all emphasize whole, unprocessed foods. Did you know overly processed foods are designed to make you crave them? Bottom line, although it's a cliché: eat the foods your grandparents would recognize.

Learn to avoid hormone disruptors. We use, and ingest, chemicals that throw our hormones off balance. Exposure to these hormone disruptors has been shown to interfere with the body's endocrine system, leading to issues with reproduction, puberty, and menopause as well as problems with the immune system and brain. Examples of hormone disruptors include pesticides, BPA, DEHP (Di[2-ethylhexyl] phthalate), dioxin, polychlorinated biphenyls, and many others. One of the best first steps can be to avoid plastics, especially heated plastics, and switch to organic produce.

Get your inflammation markers tested. Interested in your heart and overall inflammation markers? Check your cholesterol, LDL particle number and size, homocysteine, LPA, HbA1c, and fibrinogen.

Test for food intolerances. For many, this can be the missing piece of optimal health. The best part? It's totally free, and you can do it yourself. The common top offenders are:
- Cow's milk
- Eggs
- Wheat (gluten)
- Soy
- Peanuts
- Tree nuts
- Shellfish
- Corn
- MSG (and countless other preservatives)
- Sulfates

Remove each of these from your diet (one at a time) for three to four weeks and then reintroduce it. If you have a resurgence of symptoms when the foods are added back, this means that you are sensitive and you should avoid that food.

Practice gratitude. In the words of Oprah Winfrey: "Be thankful for what you have; you'll end up having more. If you concentrate on what you don't have, you will never, ever have enough."

A QUICK DEPOSIT IN YOUR WELLTH ACCOUNT

- Massage can be more than a greasy, oily, and awkward treatment—it has numerous health benefits!
- With science developing around the microbiome, the state of your gut affects almost every aspect of your overall health.
- Thoroughly check out the credentials of any doctor or practitioner before you consult with him or her.
- If something seems off about a doctor's diagnosis, don't hesitate to question him or her and seek a second opinion.

CHAPTER 10

Thank

THE ABILITY TO FEEL GRATEFUL is a huge part of enjoying satisfaction in life. If we can't feel gratitude, we're locking ourselves out of one of the most important and uplifting aspects of well-being. To say thank you—and truly mean it—is a key element of wellth.

Every day when I first wake up, I silently repeat the words *thank you* several times. The phrase is even etched on our bedroom wall, so that *thank you* is the first thing Colleen and I see when we awaken, and the last thing before we go to sleep. In addition, we have a work of art in our living room with just the word *grattitude,* from our friend Peter Tunney, the artist. (Peter likes to spell the word *gratitude* with two t's, as he says it's an attitude.) These reminders help to keep things in perspective as we go about our busy lives. Don't wait until something bad happens to you, in order to feel grateful. Gratitude should be a daily practice—not the result of a wake-up call.

There are only two ways to live your life.
One is as though nothing is a miracle.
The other is as though everything is a miracle.
—ALBERT EINSTEIN

But being grateful is something I've had to learn over my lifetime. When I was a kid, if I acted like I was feeling sorry for myself for even a moment, my mom had an immediate response. She would say to me, "The boy with no shoes cried until he met the boy with no feet." Although I sort of understood the point she was making about the power of gratitude, I still craved that toy or item of clothing. I didn't quite comprehend why I couldn't have it.

As mentioned earlier, I grew up in Manhasset, an upper-middle-class town on Long Island that was an easy commute to Manhattan; the express train was only a twenty-seven-minute ride. Filled with Wall Streeters and lawyers, the town was about 98 percent white, upper middle class, and Catholic. Most families had two parents living in a household. Looking back, it was amazing how many couples were together and not divorced. It wasn't until the early 1990s, when the recession hit, that the divorce rate skyrocketed in Manhasset. At least that was my impression, as I went from being one of the only kids with a one-parent household, to one of dozens, seemingly overnight.

As one of the few younger children who grew up in a divorced household in my neighborhood, I felt a bit out of place, as if I didn't fit in—which was ironic because I always had plenty of friends. My parents divorced when I was just three years old, so I never experienced the trauma of adults fighting that a lot of other kids go through; and I don't remember my father moving out. All I'd ever known was a home made up of my mom, my grandmother, and me. I was fine with the situation, until I discovered that everyone else had two parents at home. By then my father had remarried, and I didn't want my mom to date because I wanted her all to myself. So clearly there was nothing I could do to fix the divorce dilemma.

I was also different from my peers because I was Protestant. Every Tuesday afternoon in elementary school, when the Catholic kids went to their confirmation classes at St. Mary's, the whole building would empty out. My class population of 153 would shrink to about a dozen. Sitting alone in my empty classroom just illuminated the fact that I didn't fit in.

Finally, my family lived on the poor side of town, in a three-bedroom house with a front lawn that was about ten square feet. By Manhasset standards, it was tiny. Villages within the town of Manhasset had homes with enough acreage to play flag football. There were also country clubs like Plandome and Strathmore Vanderbilt, along with not one but *two* yacht clubs.

So I was a WASP, growing up in a small and broken home. Because of the differences between my schoolmates and me, I thought the odds were stacked against me. I would have given anything to move to one of those bigger homes in one of those nice villages, to go with everyone else to confirmation on Tuesday afternoons, and to have my parents together under one roof. I thought I had it rougher than everyone else.

I just wanted to be like them. Looking back now, I'm so glad that I wasn't, as my being different defined me in a way that I wouldn't trade for anything in the world.

I didn't begin to realize how great I had it until I was fifteen. Basketball was my passion, and I was getting pretty darn good at it. As a freshman, I was a starter on the varsity basketball team that won the county championship; in fact, I scored the go-ahead points that led to our last-minute win. Basketball was my first love, and I wanted to be the best. I desperately wanted to improve my game.

To do that, I knew I had to play with the top athletes in my age group. In some ways, I saw the game as my ticket out of Manhasset. Often we hear people reflect on their athletic success being their "ticket out" of an urban environment. My goal was the opposite: I wanted out of the posh suburbs. That meant leaving behind the cushy town with the soft white kids and going to play in Harlem at the famous Riverside Church.

After finding out when the tryouts were, I got my mom to drive me to Harlem. Back then it wasn't nearly as nice as it is now. In 1990, merely driving across 125th Street could be dangerous. After warning me to be careful, Mom dropped me off at the gate in front of the church.

In the basement of the church was a really crappy gym. It was like a death box with pillars in each corner. It was the same gym that dozens of NBA players had played in, and most of the city's best players had come through it as well. I played in that dungeon of a gym alongside everyone else. Through hard work and sweat, I made the fifteen-and-under travel team. I got another friend to join, Rob Hodgson, a great player from Long Island. Rob went on to play at Indiana, then transferred to

Rutgers. We were the only two white kids on the team. In fact, we were the only white kids on *any* of the Riverside teams—fifteen-and-under, sixteen-and-under, or seventeen-and-under.

It was during this summer that I learned the power of gratitude in a way I will never forget. That lesson has shaped my worldview perhaps more than any other experience. My greatest education to this day came from playing basketball, not classwork. I learned more about life from coaches and experiences while I was on the team than I ever did from any book.

For our first away tournament, all three age groups of the Riverside teams rode on one bus to and from Columbus, Ohio. It was a long haul, at least twelve hours each way, and we were all crammed onto the bus. I distinctly remember getting to the crappy motel rooms we were staying in. Some of my teammates were in awe of the hot water in the showers and the clean towels, things they didn't have back in the projects. We were given a per diem amount to spend on food, and usually we went to McDonald's or Burger King. I saw my teammates eating so fast, it was as if they weren't getting fed at home. Later I realized they weren't.

The first night, I put a quarter into the pay phone to call my mom and tell her I had arrived safely. One of my teammates remarked, "It's nice that you have a mom who cares where you are." I thought about that for a second, and then I said, "I know." It wasn't as if I didn't appreciate my mother, but at that moment it really hit home how lucky I was to have someone who had dedicated her life to me. I realized I was truly blessed.

Gratitude unlocks the fullness of life. It turns what we have into enough, and more. It turns denial into acceptance, chaos to order, confusion to clarity. It can turn a meal into a feast, a house into a home, a stranger into a friend.

—MELODY BEATTIE, *THE LANGUAGE OF LETTING GO*

While my world was opening up and I was learning how the other side lived, my teammates were also learning about me. A lot of these guys didn't know any other white kids. On the bus ride back, we played twenty questions. I was thrown questions like "Do you like Led Zeppelin?" or "What do you mean, you don't use lotion on your legs? What do you use?" When asked about Led Zeppelin, I replied that I liked Public Enemy. One of my teammates said, "Well, they don't like you." We both laughed.

Gratitude was slowly seeping into my veins, but it would form an indelible impression after my weeklong trip to Lubbock, Texas, a few months later for a big national tournament.

There isn't much in Lubbock except for Texas Tech University, where we played all week. We played only one game a day, when we were used to playing three or four. We were two teams of about thirty kids from Harlem with two white kids from Long Island—all of us with far too much free time in Lubbock. So one afternoon we decided to go to the mall.

Like white on rice, security guards trailed us everywhere we went. It was the first time I had witnessed racial profiling, and it hit me in a big way. It was so obvious that our group was being followed that it was uncomfortable. I could see the looks on some of my teammates' faces; some appeared shamed and embarrassed, while others were filled with a desire for vengeance. A few teammates ended up shoplifting—not because they wanted to steal something but because they were so angry at being tailed and it was their way of getting back at the guards. I understood it.

We didn't go back to the mall.

The coaches got wind of the shoplifting, and they took away our per diem for one day as punishment. If this had happened on a Manhasset traveling team, there would have been no problem. Every kid would have had extra cash from their parents; some would have had enough to support the whole team for a week. But that wasn't the case with this group. I had a little extra money, but no one else had anything, which meant they were going to starve. Some kids didn't eat, some had saved a little food, while others resorted to stealing.

I went to a 7-Eleven with one of the kids who shoplifted, and I'll never forget what a total pro he was. How calm he was, how quick, how effortlessly he took whatever food we needed. But here's the thing: this guy was a really good, sweet, and kind kid. He wasn't someone who liked stealing for the thrill of it. Afterward when we talked, he said he'd learned to steal to help make ends meet for his family. His didn't know who his father was. He had four or five brothers and sisters and a mom who worked the night shift. He also worked and went to school, and played basketball on top of everything (and he was one helluva player). He stole for survival. It wasn't a skill that he was proud of, but he needed it. I could feel the deep pain in his voice when he talked about his family and how hard things were. I could feel the shame of stealing yet the hard reality of its being necessary. I don't condone stealing, but this really opened my eyes to the fact that not everything concerning rules of conduct is cut-and-dried.

Eventually we made it out of Lubbock, and I think we even took home the championship trophy. But it's not the memory of winning, or even my first dunk in a game, that has stayed with me throughout the years. Instead, the lesson of gratitude from the experience forever changed me. From that moment on, I never let myself think that I had it worse than anyone else, or that I wasn't given a fair shake. It was clear to me that my teammates would have killed to be in my shoes.

Gratitude is the only thing that will ever make you happy. Without a doubt, if you can master the art of feeling and expressing gratitude on a daily basis, then you will have mastered happiness. It's that simple: more gratitude equals more happiness.

Think about it for a minute. The common theme behind every religion is gratitude. Whether you're Protestant, Catholic, Jewish, Muslim, or Hindu, your religion is based on the foundation of having a gratitude practice. For some people, that means a journal. For others, it's a moment of silent prayer. You can also consciously make an effort to say thank you to your partner, spouse, loved ones, or colleagues once every few days for something they've done for you. You can also do this via e-mail. There's no one-size-fits-all gratitude practice; figure out what works best for you.

Always make an effort to be grateful for what you have. No matter how bad things seem, there's someone who has it worse. It shouldn't take a traumatic life event for you to appreciate what you've lost. Instead, try to infuse gratitude into everything you do.

MR. GEORGE ON FLYING

I got really lucky with my in-laws. I love both of them, especially my father-in-law, George. "Mr. George," as I like to call him, is a character. He served two tours in Vietnam as a helicopter pilot and was shot down three times while flying. He owns a few car washes in Los Angeles and was once shot in the leg while picking up the coins from one of his locations in South Central L.A. He's also a dedicated climber (he's climbed Everest) and at age seventy, is getting into CrossFit. He's a very interesting guy who has a fascinating perspective on life.

One of my favorite George stories has to do with his take on turbulence. Colleen hates bumpy flights, but her dad has a funny way of putting it all into perspective.

George: You okay?

Colleen: I hate turbulence!

George: Is anyone shooting at us?

Colleen: What? Of course not.

George: Well, then you have nothing to worry about.

Avoid Comparing Yourself to Others

ANOTHER ASPECT OF BEING THANKFUL is avoiding comparisons. There's always someone out there who has more money, a (perceived) more perfect relationship, or a flatter stomach than you. Comparing yourself, or trying to be someone else, is a game you'll never win.

I find following this principle especially hard when it comes to business, as people are always trying to compare our company to others. In reality, this is something that's necessary. You have to measure how your product—what you're offering to your customers or readers—stacks up with the market, so you can improve the consumers' overall experience. To be honest, I really hate it. I'd rather focus entirely on being the best that we can be and let the rest take care of itself. In business, it's unavoidable, but in a personal life, you don't need to compare.

Be yourself; everyone else is taken.

—OSCAR WILDE

The legendary UCLA basketball coach John Wooden, who led the UCLA Bruins to a record ten national championships, epitomized this belief system. Unlike most basketball coaches, Wooden never considered scouting the opponent a top priority. Instead, he was more focused on getting the best out of his team.

An Easy Way to Guarantee Gratitude

IF YOU'RE EVER FEELING NEGATIVE about your life and having a tough time finding the ability to be grateful, I suggest volunteering. Go work at a soup kitchen, a battered women's shelter, or a senior citizens center. Helping others who are less fortunate is often the fastest way to gratitude. I'll never forget working at a soup kitchen in Washington, D.C., after I was feeling a bit lost personally and professionally. I had been having second thoughts about moving to a new city and leaving behind my former career and friends in New York. However, after just a few minutes of working in that kitchen, those gloomy thoughts disappeared. Instead, I counted my blessings and realized how lucky I was to be able to start over in a new place.

The more I help out, the more successful I become.
But I measure success in what it has done for the people
around me. That is the real accolade.

—ADAM GRANT, *GIVE AND TAKE*

If you're not sure where you can volunteer, take a look at organizations like Big Brothers/Big Sisters, the Salvation Army, local soup kitchens or pantries, battered women organizations, or your local church or religious organization. At the very least, charities can always use financial support—so if you don't have time right now to volunteer, you can always contribute financially.

—— Grow Your Life Savings: Thank ——

MY FRIEND DR. LISSA RANKIN believes that expressing gratitude can improve health. It seems that scientific evidence agrees with her and is conclusive when it comes to mood, outlook, and health; studies have shown that happy people live up to ten years longer than unhappy people. But how can we become happier and more optimistic in our worldview?

In *The How of Happiness,* Sonja Lyubomirsky points out that 50 percent of our propensity for happiness is based on a genetic set point; obviously, that's something we can't influence very much. Ten percent is based on life circumstances (such as getting the promotion, finding a forever soul mate, or achieving the creative dream). Forty percent is intentional activity, which we can influence through our behavior. This means that we can become up to 40 percent happier in our lives without changing our circumstances one bit, and one of the key intentional activities is the practice of gratitude.

Research shows that consistently grateful people are happier, more energetic, more hopeful, more helpful, more empathic, more spiritual, more forgiving, and less materialistic. They're also less likely to be depressed, anxious, lonely, envious, neurotic, or sick. In one study, a group of participants was asked to name five things they were grateful for every day, while another group was asked to list five things that bugged them. Those expressing gratitude were not only happier and more optimistic; they reported fewer physical symptoms (such as headache, cough, nausea, or acne).

Other gratitude studies have shown that those with chronic illnesses experience clinical improvement when practicing regular gratitude. Severely depressed people who were told to list grateful thoughts daily were found to be significantly less depressed by the end of the study, when compared to depressed people who weren't asked to express gratitude.

According to Dr. Lyubomirsky, gratitude does the following:
· Promotes savoring of positive life experiences
· Bolsters self-worth and self-esteem
· Helps people cope with stress and trauma
· Encourages caring acts and moral behavior
· Helps build social bonds, strengthen existing relationships, and nurture new relationships (and we know lonely people have twice the rate of heart disease as those with strong social connections)
· Inhibits harmful comparisons
· Diminishes or deters negative feelings such as anger, bitterness, and greed
· Thwarts hedonistic adaptation (the ability to adjust your set point to positive new circumstances so that we don't appreciate the new circumstance and it has little affect on our overall health or happiness)

Here are some ways that you can practice gratitude:

Keep a gratitude journal. Ponder three to five things you're currently grateful for. (It's okay if they're mundane things!) Write them down. Data suggest that doing this even once per week may be beneficial. If you find that doing it daily works for you, go for it!

For a heart-opening twist on the gratitude journal, try the Three Question Journal developed by Angeles Arrien and taught to medical students and physicians around the globe by Rachel Naomi Remen, M.D. At the end of the day, take a moment to think backward through your day and ask yourself three questions:

- What surprised me today?
- What touched my heart today?
- What inspired me today?

Making the Three Question Journal a daily practice bench-presses your gratitude muscles; it increases your ability to be surprised, touched, and inspired by even the smallest acts of kindness, beauty, and love. Before you know it, your heart gets cracked open, and love starts to spill out all over your life.

Train your brain. Journaling may not be your cup of tea, so you may be better off just training yourself to think grateful thoughts. Try noticing one ungrateful thought you have each day, and try switching it around to something for which you can be grateful. For instance, if you complain about your daily commute, instead try to be grateful that you have a job.

Vary your gratitude practice. In addition to journaling or thinking grateful thoughts, speak up about what you're grateful for at dinnertime, make art about what you're lucky to have, but shake it up! We tend to get bored easily, so the practice of gratitude works better when we change how we're grateful.

Express gratitude directly to others. Call a friend, write a letter, share your grateful thoughts with family members, or speak to a colleague at work. There's no upper limit to who you can thank for their contributions to your life.

A QUICK DEPOSIT IN YOUR WELLTH ACCOUNT

- A great way to become more thankful is to keep a daily gratitude journal. Each day write down one thing you're grateful for.
- You can't be wellthy unless you're able to feel grateful.
- Don't compare yourself to others. That's a game you can't win. There will always be someone smarter, richer, thinner, or more successful. Instead, be happy for what you have.
- Giving does even more for the donor or volunteer than it does for the recipient.

CHAPTER 11

Ground

IT HAS BECOME CLEARER TO me over the years that a connection with nature is supremely important to our overall wellth. That's why my company is named mindbodygreen, the *green* implying ecological awareness and being in touch with the earth.

Before mindbodygreen launched, phrases like *mind-body spirit, mind-body soul,* and *mind-body connection* were all pretty common. Before I had my epiphany, I thought the only word that mattered within those three was the body: if you looked good in the mirror, then you were all set—not only with yourself but with the opposite sex. Boy, was I wrong. To live our healthiest lives, we need a three-pronged approach, focusing on mind, body, and green. Whether we like it or not, everything is connected: our minds, our bodies, and our environment.

Let me explain. The mind and body are not separate; they're one. That's why we could read every book in the self-help section and follow someone else's rigid rules to lose weight but still be unhealthy. If we're out of touch with our body, then we're not truly healthy, because we're disconnected from our self.

So let's say that we've nailed the mind-body part: we have

a spiritual practice, we're expressing gratitude on a daily basis, we're meditating, we're doing yoga, we're eating more plants, and we're eating organic. Does this mean we're healthy? Well, maybe—or maybe not. There's another piece of the health puzzle: the green part.

Two questions I encourage us all to ask ourselves: What are we putting into our homes and our bodies? Are we putting chemicals and toxins into them, or are we using natural products? Chemicals and toxins can easily negate all that good work we're doing with our spiritual and physical development.

The state of our health reflects the food we eat, the exercise we take, the water we drink, the air we breathe, and the quality of our housing and sanitation. I believe it also extends to our social needs and circumstances—the need to belong to a community, the need for meaningful work, and daily purpose. The need in our lives for dignity and kindness, for self-respect, for hope, and, above all, for harmony and, dare I say it, beauty. It encompasses the power of art, the healing properties of loving human relationships, and the role of the human spirit. Human health is a sum of all these parts.

—PRINCE CHARLES

Do you have a connection to nature? No matter what your religion (if you have any at all), you can make the argument that we all come from the same source and that we're all connected to each other. Our environment comes from this same place, or creator. So doesn't that mean we should treat our environment with respect? Ultimately, it's what unifies and supports us all.

So there you have it, mindbodygreen. Not three words; one word. Mindbodygreen is all connected, and I believe it's the true solution to health and wellth.

Thousands of tired, nerve-shaken, over-civilized people are beginning to find out that going to the mountains is going home; that wildness is a necessity; and that mountain parks and reservations are useful not only as fountains of timber and irrigating rivers, but as fountains of life.

—JOHN MUIR, *OUR NATIONAL PARKS*

As I've gotten older, I've found that I almost crave nature when I don't get it. I'm a New Yorker, and I usually prefer walking in a city over hiking in a forest. In the past few years I've found it really refreshing to walk barefoot in the sand or on grass. In some circles this process is called grounding, but it just means doing something many of us did as kids: walking barefoot on sand, grass, soil, or any natural surface.

Scientific research suggests that there are numerous benefits to grounding. In a 2012 study of the many benefits of this practice, the researchers concluded that they have to do with the connection between our bodies and Earth's electrons:

Emerging scientific research has revealed a surprisingly positive and overlooked environmental factor on health: direct physical contact with the vast supply of electrons on the surface of the Earth. Modern lifestyle separates humans from such contact. The research suggests that this disconnect may be a major contributor to physiological dysfunction and unwellness. Reconnection with the Earth's electrons has been found to promote intriguing physiological changes and subjective reports of well-being. Earthing (or grounding) refers to the discovery of benefits—including better sleep and reduced pain—from walking barefoot outside.

Regardless of what the studies say, I just love how it feels! Walking barefoot on soft white (and clean) sand is one of my absolute favorite things to do. I find myself craving this every few months, especially in the winter. I travel a lot to the West Coast for work, and whenever I have the opportunity, I'll try to get to the beach or a park, take off my sneakers, and walk barefoot for a little bit. Even if I only have a few minutes, I try to be very mindful about each and every step as I feel my feet sinking into the ground. I find the practice of grounding very therapeutic. And it's something that this native New Yorker would never in a million years have guessed I'd love!

What we've been given here is precious: majestic in its smallest details and its grandest spectacles. Anytime you feel in danger of forgetting that, I recommend you take a good look at a 50 foot wave. Anyone who can be around something that powerful and not feel humbled has some serious analyzing to do.

—LAIRD HAMILTON, *FORCE OF NATURE*

Green Homes

BEING GREEN INCLUDES AVOIDING TOXINS in your home. It isn't easy to be entirely chemical-free, but it's worth trying to weed out unnecessary products that can be substituted for natural ones, such as nontoxic cleaning supplies.

Here's some science that might catch your attention. A 2009 study conducted by the Environmental Working Group (EWG) found up to 232 toxic chemicals in the umbilical blood cord samples from ten newborn babies:

> Besides BPA, substances detected for the first time in U.S. newborns included a toxic flame retardant chemical called tetrabromobisphenol A (TBBPA) that permeates computer circuit boards, synthetic fragrances used in common cosmetics and detergents, and perfluorobutanoic acid, a member of the notorious Teflon chemical family used to make non-stick and grease-, stain- and water-resistant coatings for cookware, textiles, food packaging and other consumer products.

All this in newborn babies! Imagine what some years on this earth would add to that collection. This study alone—and there are others showing similar findings—should convince anyone that green is the color of health.

Most of us don't realize that the products we use every day can expose us to thousands of chemicals that are readily absorbed through our skin. The impact on your health? It's not pretty.

—SIOBHAN O'CONNOR AND ALEXANDRA SPUNT,
NO MORE DIRTY LOOKS

My friend Heather White, executive director of the Environmental Working Group, has a lot to say about how to reduce your exposure to chemicals.

Three Easy Ways to Shop Greener

Here are three great tips for shopping smarter and reducing your exposure to toxic chemicals:

1. **Read the labels.** Most of us focus on labels when we're buying food, but have you ever taken a look at the ingredient labels on your personal care or cleaning products? Although they can be confusing, just learning a few chemical names to watch out for, like *triclosan*, *parabens*, and *phthalates*, can empower you to avoid the worst potential offenders and protect your health.

2. **Research before you buy.** The Environmental Working Group, the nonprofit environmental health organization I run, has created some great tools to help you shop smarter. Look

up personal care products using EWG's Skin Deep Database (www.ewg.org/skindeep), or check out which additives may be lurking in your favorite "healthy" packaged foods and find better alternatives using EWG's Food Scores (www.ewg.org/food scores). Both of these tools are available as iPhone or Android apps. EWG's consumer guides cover a wide range of topics that are easy to use and understand so you can feel empowered to make smarter, healthier, and greener choices for yourself and your family.

3. **Opt for simple and homemade.** Changing your cleaning and beauty routines is much easier than you think. DIY products are fun to make and can be as effective as and cheaper than store-bought varieties. Try using vinegar and baking soda as an all-natural drain cleaner or replacing your moisturizer with organic coconut butter. Also try opting for products with a shorter ingredient list, as fewer ingredients means less risk of exposure to questionable toxic chemicals.

—— Grow Your Life Savings: Ground ——

DR. PATRICIA THOMPSON IS A corporate psychologist, life coach, and author. Here she discusses the health benefits of spending time in nature.

Appreciating the magnificence of trees, inhaling salty ocean air, or marveling at the colors of a field of flowers always fills me with a sense of wonder and renews my spirit. There's a good reason why so many artists and poets have found inspiration in the beauty of creation. Research has shown that spending time in nature can benefit you both mentally and physically, in a variety of surprising ways.

Spending time in nature increases your sense of vitality. A series of studies examined the effects of nature on participants' self-reported levels of vitality. The researchers found that spending time in nature, looking at pictures of it, and even visualizing nature scenes increased participants' energy. It's no surprise: when you're outside, you're surrounded by the sights, sounds, and smells of life. In the midst of all of this stimulation of the senses, how could you help but feel more alive?

Taking in nature makes you more resilient to stress. In one study, participants were shown a traumatic video of workplace accidents followed by a video that showed either outdoor scenes of nature or urban environments. Researchers found that the individuals who viewed the nature scenes showed faster physical recovery from the effects of stress than the subjects who had looked at urban scenes. So, if you're feeling overwhelmed and need a break, talking a walk in the park or even resting on your deck looking at the trees is bound to relax and renew you.

Exercising in nature enhances your mood. It's a pretty commonly known fact that exercise produces endorphins, which are the body's natural mood enhancers. And when you add nature to the equation, these effects are compounded. For example, a review of several studies showed that exercising outdoors improved participants' moods and self-esteem after a mere five minutes. For extra benefit, exercise somewhere around water, as this was found to have an even greater effect. Swimming or running on the beach, anyone?

Being in nature helps with focus. Research has shown that spending time in nature is associated with enhanced concentration. For example, one study discovered that children who were diagnosed with ADHD showed better concentration after taking a twenty-minute walk in nature, compared to a walk in an urban setting. Another study showed that taking a walk in the park (or even just looking at green space) helped increase participants' abilities to concentrate and relieve brain fatigue. So instead of a dose of caffeine, why not take a dose of nature? It helps as a brain pick-me-up without any side effects!

Living near green space can improve your mental health. One study that followed participants for a five-year period found that moving to an area that has more green space was associated with greater well-being among the participants. And believe it or not, this effect lasted for three years. This should definitely give city planners something to think about if they want to enhance population health.

Spending time in nature can boost your immune system. Researchers have found that spending time in nature increases your sense of awe (e.g., that feeling of reverence and respect you get as a result of being overwhelmed by the majesty of a mountain or the beauty of a sunset). Not only does awe make you more aware of the present moment and increase your life satisfaction, it is also linked to lower levels of cytokines, which are markers of inflammation.

Exposure to nature can also make you more generous. As another example of the awesomeness of awe, research has also shown that people who experience awe on a regular basis are more inclined to be generous to strangers. In one study, students who had the awe-inspiring experience of spending time in a beautiful grove of trees were more likely to help someone who had a minor accident than other students who had spent a similar period of time looking at a building. The researchers argued that awe fills us with a feeling of connection to others, in that we see ourselves as part of a larger whole.

Living near green space may even increase your life span. A five-year study of senior citizens in Japan showed that living near areas with walkable green spaces was associated with a decreased risk of death during the study. This relationship was found even after controlling for variables like income, age, sex, marital status, and other relevant factors. Want to live longer? Move near a park!

Having indoor plants can positively affect your health. Even if you're unable to spend a lot of time outdoors, bringing nature inside can also benefit you. For example, a study of hospital patients recovering from surgery found that individuals who were put in rooms with plants exhibited lower blood pressure and heart rate, lower ratings of pain, anxiety, and fatigue, and took fewer doses of pain medication compared to a control group.

The takeaways? Surround yourself with greenery. Have plants indoors, and take the amount of green space into account when selecting a place to live. Get outside in nature as much as possible. If you can be around water, even better. And finally, keep in mind the words of Anne Frank: "The best remedy for those who are afraid, lonely, or unhappy is to go outside, somewhere where they can be quite alone with the heavens, nature and God. Because only then does one feel that all is as it should be, and that God wishes to see people happy, amidst the simple beauty of nature."

A QUICK DEPOSIT IN YOUR WELLTH ACCOUNT

- Nature offers a break and a balm. Try to schedule regular breaks in which you take in the beauty of the natural world.
- Grounding is an easy way to appreciate being in touch with the earth.

- Where possible, detoxify your home, including cleaning supplies, and especially personal care products and cosmetics!
- Use resources like the Environmental Working Group's Skin Deep database to find clean personal care products.

CHAPTER 12

Live

ANOTHER IMPORTANT FACET OF LIVING a life of wellth is being aware that life does come to an end. We've been told that we should all live each day as if it could be our last, but sometimes it takes the death of a loved one to bring this lesson home in a very real way.

It was a crisp spring morning in March 1994, and I was massively hungover from a keg party the previous night. You know by now that at nineteen, partying was definitely my top priority. I was supposed to drive from Long Island to Westchester to watch my father play paddle tennis, a game similar to tennis but with a smaller court and a solid racket. But I wanted to sleep in, so I blew him off. When I called to make my excuses, he was hurt and upset.

I was mad at my dad for being so angry. After all, he wasn't always there for me. Although I was incredibly close to my mother and grandmother, with whom I lived, my relationship with my father for a long time was distant at best.

The past year had been different, though. He was more present than he'd ever been. Typically I'd see him once or twice a month, either at my basketball games or at games that we went to together. But now he came to all my games, and we'd grab dinner afterward and have real conversations. Finally we were in a good place. Ironically, he was flat broke after going belly-up in the collapse of the commercial real estate market.

He easily could have been depressed, frantic, or at the very least preoccupied. Instead, his priorities seemed to have changed, and I was now one of them. A few days after blowing off his game, I called him and apologized. We said very little, but it was clear that our anger had dissipated. I said I loved him, and we moved on.

Just a few days later, he died suddenly.

I'll never forget that afternoon. I was pulling into our driveway with my friend Matt after a trip to Tower Records. I saw the look on my mother's face, and I knew something was very wrong. At the age of forty-six, my father had suffered a massive heart attack and died instantly—right before a paddle tennis game.

Our friends and family couldn't understand how someone who looked so healthy and was so physically fit could die in an instant from a massive heart attack. Here was a man who could pass for someone in his late thirties. He participated in hundred-plus-mile bike races, and just that previous year he had won the national doubles paddle tennis championship for forty-five-and-under.

My father was born with some heart issues, but he never took his heart problem seriously, even though he'd had a few warning signs like palpitations and even a minor heart attack while in jail.

Yes, he was in jail, and this is where stress comes into the story. He had just gone though a very bitter divorce with his second wife, while at the same time his real estate business collapsed. Overnight my dad went from being a high-flyer to practically broke. Some of it was due to the real estate collapse in the early 1990s, and some of it was his fault. He was a spender, not a saver. He couldn't spend money fast enough, from cars to boats to vacations. He lived life only one way: at full speed and to the max.

There's something I have to respect about that attitude, but it's also reckless and irresponsible. And when the music stopped, his finances collapsed, and so did his marriage. It's funny how money can sometimes patch up marital problems, but once the supply of cash goes, it's as if the levee has broken, and a flood of problems drown the relationship.

During the divorce proceedings, my father agreed to pay a very expensive alimony. Initially he could afford it, but as the market and his finances began to dwindle, he couldn't. Still, my father was the type of guy who, no matter how bad things got, always thought he could turn it around. It didn't matter that he was in debt, and there wasn't a chance in hell he'd make a comeback.

When the alimony came due, he couldn't make the payments, and he was thrown in jail.

That's where he was when he had his first palpitations and heart attack. He never let on that he was anxious about his business or personal life, but it became clear to those closest to him that the stress was hitting him hard. After he died, we all believed that stress was the major culprit.

In the midst of my shock and sadness, one of the first things that came to mind was how much more devastated I would have been if we had never made up. What if I hadn't called him to apologize? We still would have been upset with each other and never would have had the chance to repair our relationship and acknowledge the love that had recently flourished between us.

Since then I never leave or hang up on an angry note with a loved one. I'm almost obsessed with closing every text, every e-mail, every conversation with those I care about—especially with my wife and my mother—with an "I love you." No matter how mad either of us is at the other, "I love you" are my closing words. I see it as a gift from my father, my first hard-won lesson about loss. This simple practice has deepened my connections with those I care about most. If I lose them, at least they will know how much I loved them.

Death ends a life, not a relationship.
—MITCH ALBOM, *TUESDAYS WITH MORRIE*

After my dad died, I cried nonstop for two days. Yet at his funeral I had a sense of being profoundly connected to him, and this felt surprisingly good. I experienced a euphoric sense of joy and an unfamiliar spiritual understanding, a simple knowing that everything was all right. While I was grateful for this unexpected knowledge, I couldn't help but think that it was incredibly bizarre. I actually felt happiness at my father's funeral? This was my second lesson about death: that despite the pain, it can be as much about connection as it is about loss.

Mourning my father birthed a new sense of faith in spirit and a belief that loved ones can inform and enrich your life even when they're gone. That set the stage for so many changes to come. I'm not sure I would have had the courage to eventually leave a conventional career and launch a new business, or to take up yoga or meditation, if I hadn't experienced the opening up I did at that time. I also learned that I could survive even the deepest hurt and emerge with a sense of peace.

It's so much darker when a light goes out than it would have been if it had never shone.

—JOHN STEINBECK, *THE WINTER OF OUR DISCONTENT*

Eight years after my father's death came a very different kind of loss. Tim O'Loughlin was one of my oldest and closest friends. I lost him when he was twenty-eight years old, and his death was nothing less than devastating. Tim had been plagued with bipolar disorder for most of his life. But he had recently visited me in Washington, D.C., to go to a Rolling Stones concert, and we'd had a fantastic time. Tim and I talked almost every week, and he was always quite candid about how he was feeling. He seemed to be on his way back up. Things were coming together for him—his relationships, his career, his perspective on life. So when I got the call that his father had found him dead, I was in complete shock.

Having made it through my father's funeral without shedding a tear, I thought I'd have a similar experience at Tim's wake. Boy, was I wrong. As soon as I pulled up to the parking lot of the funeral home, I lost it. I was crying hysterically, as my mother held me. Finally I got it together and went inside, but as soon as I made eye contact with Tim's mother, Kathy, we both began to cry uncontrollably.

The next day when I eulogized Tim, I burst into sobs that I could barely control—three separate times. I cried more at Tim's wake and funeral than I did when my father died. Where was that sense of serenity and peace now? His loss felt meaningless, and for months afterward a kind of existential depression colored everything I did.

At a certain point, I began to think something was really wrong with me. Now I know that there wasn't. Losing a best friend who was my own age felt tragic in an entirely different way from the loss of my father. I had thought our friendship would last forever, and also I was confronted with an aching awareness of my own mortality.

When I emerged from that acute stage of grieving, I began to feel a sense of urgency about identifying and achieving my goals. I got moving. I learned that the most painful losses can shock you out of complacency and clarify your life in bold relief. That was my gift from Tim.

This kind of clarity is something we all need, whether or not we've lost a loved one. Cherish each day of life as the gift that it is. Be aware that you can lose a loved one in a heartbeat, and treat them accordingly. This is not to say that we have to walk around with a cloud over our heads or dwell on constant morbid thoughts. But being aware of the fleeting quality of life can lead to a heightened appreciation of everyday experience. This can be the final linchpin in acquiring wellth.

Life is simple. Everything happens for you, not to you.
Everything happens at exactly the right moment,
neither too soon nor too late. You don't have to like it . . .
it's just easier if you do.

—BYRON KATIE, *LOVING WHAT IS*

Then nine years later my grandmother died. Once again grief took me by surprise. I was overwhelmed by the seemingly endless pain of her loss. At the age of ninety-one, her death was the most natural, and yet to me it was the most devastating. My maternal grandmother had been like a second mother to me. I grew up in the same house with her—just me, my mom, and my grandma. We ate meals together, we watched TV together, and we traveled together. I even got her practicing yoga at ninety.

At first, the diagnosis of metastasized cancer was hard to believe. She was so limber and vital, moving faster than anyone I knew. To my shock, within weeks of the diagnosis, the cancer had progressed to its final stage. I crawled into her hospital bed and cried as silently as I could. Every time I hugged her, I tried to be as fully present as possible, not thinking about anything else other than how that hug felt, feeling her energy, hearing her voice, trying to absorb every moment. I loved her so much that it hurt.

I basically cried for four months, from the time of her diagnosis until she passed away. Watching her die in such excruciating pain was almost unbearable. Although I tried to console myself with the knowledge that she had had a full life, I felt a hole in my own existence, and I still feel it to this day.

Acceptance is not defeat. Acceptance is just awareness.
—STEPHEN COLBERT, GQ

Losing my grandmother when I was thirty-seven felt nothing like losing my best friend at twenty-eight, or my father at age nineteen. Along with that loss came another lesson: every death is different, and everyone deals with death differently. There's no playbook for grieving, and there's certainly no right or wrong way to do it. I've learned to let myself grieve fully, no matter how much I'd rather move on or how surprising or off-putting I find my reactions at first. It may sound like a cliché, but grieving is a way of honoring ourselves and the deceased, no matter what that grief looks like. There's no way around grieving—you can only go through it.

Research has shown that even when people are in the throes of sadness or tears, they may still be able to laugh or smile as they remember their loved one. Mourners who can experience moments of happiness or humor recover from acute grief far more quickly than those who cannot. Even when things are challenging, try to seek out some joy that can seep in. And as mentioned in the previous chapter, a gratitude practice can help to balance out the depth of pain that you're experiencing.

After a while, nonstop mourning can become draining. I recall sitting around the O'Loughlins' house after Tim's funeral with a bunch of my close friends from high school, all of us extremely upset and trying to make sense of how we could lose someone so young. Then one friend recalled one of the many dumb and entertaining moments we'd shared with Tim just a few years before. We all laughed. And that story led to the next tale and the next, and so on. An hour later we had gone from tears of sadness to tears of laughter and appreciation, as we celebrated a dear friend's short but meaningful life.

On the death of a friend, we should consider that the fates through confidence have devolved on us the task of a double living, that we have henceforth to fulfill the promise of our friend's life also, in our own, to the world.

—HENRY DAVID THOREAU, *JOURNAL*, VOL. 1

Coping with the death of a loved one is never easy, and I've learned that there's no right or wrong way to grieve. But I also believe in the circle of life, meaning that if something dies, it gives life to another being. For every ending, there's a new beginning. I don't believe in reincarnation; instead, I believe that mortality makes us confront the reality of our own lives and address things that need to be changed. Life is precious, and it can be taken away without a moment's notice. It's important to never lose sight of the miracle we are all living every day.

—— Grow Your Life Savings: Live ——

SPEAKER AND AUTHOR OF *Keep Going: From Grief to Growth,* Aimee DuFresne has helped me understand so much about how grief has shaped my life, and about how to help others going through a loss. I asked her to share her hard-won wisdom about how to react to a person who is grieving.

— WHAT NEVER TO SAY TO SOMEONE IN MOURNING —

It's hard to know what to say to someone who has lost a loved one. So many grieving people have told me how painful it was when, in an attempt to comfort them, friends and acquaintances inadvertently said words that left them feeling empty or even more bereft. Of course, these words were spoken with the best of intentions, but they were way off the mark. Here are some tips to keep in mind the next time you're in the presence of someone in mourning.

"Everything happens for a reason." This is the last thing a newly grieving person needs to hear. Don't get me wrong: I totally believe it's true. I live my life by it. But when unexpected tragedy strikes, most of us experience the senselessness of death. We need to recalibrate. Reassess. Reset.

Not long after I started college, a high school friend's dad died suddenly. She had been one of the most positive people I knew. Her whole life was planned out perfectly. College. Marriage.

Two kids. That girl had it down, and I was in awe. So I was taken aback when I spoke to her right after she lost her dad. She told me she had always thought everything happened for a reason, but this loss proved her wrong. She went on to inform me that she was quitting college—she had only enrolled to make her dad proud anyway, so what was the point? She no longer wanted to marry—who would walk her down the aisle? Having kids was out of the question; she didn't want to put anyone else through the pain of losing a parent.

When I ran into her again years later, I shouldn't have been surprised that she'd decided to stay in school. After she'd graduated, she'd gotten married and given birth to two beautiful girls. Once again, that girl had it down.

Would it have helped if, at the time of her dad's death, I had reassured her that everything happened for a reason; that she would get back on track? Not at all. She needed time to think, heal, and decide for herself when and how she wanted to go on with her life. We all need that time.

"Time heals all wounds." Oh, really? How much time exactly? Weeks? Months? Years? Decades? Centuries? Here's the truth: time does not heal. I realize that this goes against the common wisdom about loss. But there's good news: time does change us. My friend who lost her dad said that she continued to feel the pain of his loss, but a year later she was no longer paralyzed by it. She got going again. She went back to college and moved forward with fulfilling her dreams, in honor of her father as well as herself.

"You're young. You'll find someone else." If you've ever said this to someone grieving the loss of their life partner, I urge you to get on the phone today and apologize profusely for being so blasé. Ask your friend for forgiveness. Then forgive yourself and make a pledge never to say this again.

"Are you over it yet?" or "It's been over a year . . ." I cannot tell you how many people asked me a variation of the first question after my first husband, Ben, passed away. The first time came after one month! A year later the same question began coming my way again. One day a good friend asked that insensitive question: "It's been over year. Do you feel over it yet?" "No! I don't!" I shouted in disbelief. She shrugged, seemingly annoyed by my inability to heal as quickly as she thought I should.

Surprisingly, it was more painful for me to hear the question a year or even years after my husband's death. Why? By then the shock had fully worn off, and the fact that I had to rebuild my life alone had fully kicked in. Meanwhile the friends who thought I was over it were checking out, assuming I was healed. It's safe to say that no one gets over the loss of a life partner, a child, a parent, or a close friend. Again, most of us, like my high school friend, will choose to go on with our lives, and many of us will find happiness and love again, but the pain of our loss will always be with us.

The best thing to say to someone in mourning is simple and sweet: "I love you."

At the time of Ben's passing, it had been almost two years since I had spoken to my mother. When we'd been in touch, she hadn't always said what I wanted to hear. In fact, sometimes she said the complete opposite. (Perhaps you can relate.) Just after Ben died, she called. I braced myself for the worst, but I felt too weak to defend myself against any unwanted words.

I needn't have worried. In that moment, my mom, after about a thirty-year run of saying the wrong thing, blew me away by saying what I so desperately needed to hear: "I love you." And she kept saying it, over and over. It was heartfelt. It was healing. It was helpful when no other words came close. And it gave me a glimpse of ease in the midst of incredible pain.

When you meet someone who has lost someone, instead of asking about the details of that person's death, why not ask something different, like:

- *What was their name?*
- *What did they love to do?*
- *How did they inspire you?*
- *Do you feel their presence since their passing?*

Focus on the life, rather than the loss. It might make all the difference.

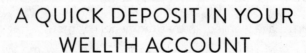

A QUICK DEPOSIT IN YOUR WELLTH ACCOUNT

- Live each day as if it could be your last. This attitude can give everyday experiences new meaning.
- Even in the midst of mourning a loved one, a little laughter or a smile can provide a bit of relief.
- Never tell someone who is mourning, "Time heals all wounds." Instead, simply offer your love and support.
- There's no right or wrong way to grieve. We have to go through grief in our own way.
- Respect the right of others to mourn in the way they need to, and accept your own reactions to your loss.

CHAPTER 13

Laugh

WHEN I WAS SEVENTEEN AND being recruited to play basketball at Columbia, head coach Jack Rohan visited me and my mother to make his pitch. We actually didn't talk a lot about basketball—Jack mostly told stories that had us rolling in laughter. One was about an Irish funeral he had attended recently, where many of the guests got so drunk they took the body out of the casket and started taking pictures with the corpse. I found out later from assistant coach Paul Lee, who was with Jack on the visit, that right after he left the house, he turned to Paul and said, "I don't know if we're going to get the kid to come to Columbia, but we sure had a few good laughs."

I'll also never forget the story of one of my good childhood friends who was running late to work. After realizing he didn't have his subway pass and seeing a long line, he decided to hop the turnstile. As luck would have it, two plainclothes police officers saw it and arrested him. He didn't have ID on him, so they brought him down to the precinct. My friend was very likable and charming. The next thing you know, the arresting officers had called his boss to say that he had helped them apprehend a criminal and would be late to work. When my friend arrived to the office later that morning, it was to a standing ovation.

Life and laughter isn't about getting piss-drunk, making poor decisions, and then laughing about them (although there's definitely some humor in those situations). And it's not about turning lemons into lemonade by turning arrests into standing ovations. Instead, life and laughter are what keep us going through the hard times.

Sometimes life can really suck. It's not all unicorns and rainbows and it's not filled with organic, gluten-free cookies that also happen to be sugar-free, vegan, *and* delicious (I've yet to find such a cookie but if you find it, please let me know!). There are major detours and potholes—such as death, disease, and backbreaking financial hardship—that can be debilitating. But no matter how hard things are, we must believe that our situation can get better. And most of the time things aren't even all that bad; we're just wound so tight that we can't find the humor in some of the potholes.

Life moves pretty fast. If you don't stop and look around once in a while, you could miss it.

—FERRIS BUELLER, *FERRIS BUELLER'S DAY OFF*

One of my first lessons in laughter occurred as I was fast pursuing wealth, as opposed to wellth. It was early in my career during the summer of 2000, when I had my first really bad day as a trader on Wall Street. I lost a ton of money, which basically wiped out most of my month's profit. I felt like an idiot, and I was so upset with myself. A friend and fellow trader, who was one of the best at the firm, saw how distraught I was. He turned to me and said, "This is the first time you lost a shitload of money, but it won't be the last. If you're any good at trading, it'll happen again. In fact, you'll lose a lot more. But you'll win a lot more, too. So get used to it."

He smiled and walked away. And he was right; I did lose more, and I did win more. I learned to laugh at my losses, knowing they would right themselves later. But eventually I won more—not by pursuing wealth but by pursuing wellth. Winning in wellth is not measured by any scorecard, and success does not particularly look like anything or anyone. Wellth is a state of being that is indescribable, malleable, and constantly changing with you. You and only you define it. You were born wellthy, and it's time to return to that state of being. Your version of wellth will be 100 percent unique to you, and you'll 100 percent know what it looks and feels like when you get there.

I hope you begin your journey to wellth today. Try using the preceding chapters to make deposits into your wellth account: Eat. Move. Work. Believe. Explore. Breathe. Feel. Love. Heal. Thank. Ground. Live. And last but not least—Laugh. Because after all, if we can't find humor in this zigzagging journey called life, then what are we here for?

ACKNOWLEDGMENTS

THANK YOU TO MY AMAZING team at mindbodygreen, starting with my incredibly talented cofounders: Tim Glenister, who can build anything; Carver Anderson, who does anything and everything no matter how big or small the task; Kerry Shaw, my sister-in-law/editor in chief extraordinaire who is a genius when it comes to content; my wife and wellness muse Colleen; and to the entire team at mindbodygreen. You all make me look good. Please continue to do so!

I'm eternally grateful to the mindbodygreen community of readers, watchers, contributors, and partners, many of whom have been with us from the start when we were running on pure passion. Your friendship and support mean the world to me. And special thanks to the mbg supporters who contributed to this book!

Thank you to my small, yet incredibly supportive and loving family for always being there for me. I could write an entire book about how grateful I am for having such a loving and supportive mother. A special shout-out goes to my in-laws Alyse and George for not just being amazing in-laws, but for the best espresso west of the Mississippi.

Acknowledgments

To all my friends from Manhasset, Northfield Mount Hermon, Columbia, Heartland Securities, and various teams, jobs, and cities along the way: you know who you are. I'm filled with enough great memories to last a lifetime.

Thank you to Linda Loewenthal, whose snail mail and persistence led to this book; to Leslie Wells for working with my penchant for run-on sentences; to my brilliant editor at Penguin Random House, Heather Jackson, for believing in and shaping this big idea called wellth; and to the entire team at Penguin Random House for supporting this book!

I've played for more bad coaches than good coaches in my athletic career, but let's finish on a positive note with two who had a lasting impact on me. To Bill Batty, who epitomizes what wellth is; and to Armond Hill, who I find myself quoting more and more as I get older.

Thank you to Dr. Frank Lipman, Sam Berlind, and Joyce George for keeping all 79 inches of me in tip-top physical and spiritual shape!

And to all my friends and family, past, present, and future—it's because of all of you that I consider myself to be wellthy.

Last, but certainly not least, thank you to my father, who I'm sure was the guardian angel who kept my poor decision making in my twenties from turning into a disaster.

Chapter 1: Eat

12   *"Someone has to stand up":* Bill Maher, on *Real Time with Bill Maher,* Sept. 28, 2007.

13   *"You can't expect to live":* Kris Carr, interview on mindbodygreen.com, June 28, 2010.

Chapter 2: Move

29   *"You can be unbelievably fit":* Rich Roll, interview on mindbodygreen.com, June 21, 2010.

Chapter 3: Work

48   *"Happy is harder than money":* David Geffen, interview on *20/20,* April 22, 1994.

50   *"Everywhere we look in business":* Steven Kotler, "Create a Work Environment that Fosters Flow," *Harvard Business Review,* May 6, 2014.

Chapter 4: Believe

62   *"individuals with the highest levels":* Rosalba Hernandez, quoted in Laura Stamper, "How Optimism Might Be Good for Your Heart," *Time,* Jan. 12, 2015.

77   *"Visualization works":* Jim Carrey, *The Oprah Winfrey Show,*
      June 4, 2009.

Chapter 5: Explore

89   *"A master in the art of living":* Lawrence Pearsall Jacks,
      Education Through Recreation (New York: Harper & Bros.,
      1932), p. 1.

90   *"A man is a success":* Jonathan Cott, *Bob Dylan: The Essential
      Interviews* (New York: Wenner, 2006), p. 291.

94   *"I like money":* Seinfeld quoted in Jonah Weiner, "Jerry
      Seinfeld Intends to Die Standing Up," *New York Times
      Magazine,* Dec. 20, 2012.

Chapter 7: Feel

117   *Centre for Ageing Studies at Flinders University:* The study
      followed nearly 1,500 older people for ten years. It found
      that those who had a large network of friends outlived those
      with the fewest friends by 22 percent. In 1989 David Spiegel,
      M.D., a professor of psychiatry at Stanford University,
      published a landmark paper in *Lancet* that showed that
      women with breast cancer who participated in a support
      group lived twice as long as those who didn't. They also had
      much less pain. Tom Valeo, "Good Friends Are Good for
      You," *WebMD,* Jan. 2007, http://wb.md/1dAeG3s.

118   *Dunbar's Number:* Here's a great article if you're interested in
      learning more about Dunbar's Number: Maria Konnikova,
      "The Limits of Friendship," *New Yorker,* Oct. 7, 2014.

Chapter 9: Heal

159   *"When health is absent":* Herophilus, *The Art of Medicine
      in Early Alexandria,* ed. and trans. Heinrich von Staden
      (Cambridge, UK: Cambridge University Press, 2007).

162   *"The doctor of the future"*: "Wizard Edison," *Newark Advocate*
       (Jan. 2, 1903), p. 1, quoted in Barbara Mikkelson and David
       P. Mikkelson, "The Doctor of the Future," Snopes.com,
       Jan. 25, 2015.

167   *researchers studied 263 volunteers:* A. D. Kaye et al., "The
       Effect of Deep-Tissue Massage Therapy on Blood Pressure
       and Heart Rate," *Journal of Alternative and Complementary
       Medicine* 14, no. 2 (2008): 125–28, doi: 10.1089/
       acm.2007.0665.

167   *backed up these findings:* Mahshid Givi, "Durability of Effect
       of Massage Therapy on Blood Pressure," *International
       Journal of Preventive Medicine* 4, no. 5 (May 2013): 511–16,
       PMC3733180.

167   *drop in markers of inflammation:* Izreen Supa'at et al., "Effects
       of Swedish Massage Therapy on Blood Pressure, Heart
       Rate, and Inflammatory Markers in Hypertensive Women,"
       Evidence-Based Complementary and Alternative Medicine
       (2013), doi: 10.1155/2013/171852.

168   *"Improvements in the ability . . . in research studies":* Arnt V.
       Kristen et al. "Acupuncture Improves Exercise Tolerance
       of Patients with Heart Failure: A Placebo-Controlled
       Pilot Study." *Heart* 96 (2010): 1396–1400, doi:10.1136/
       hrt.2009.187930.

168   *"More than three thousand":* Y. M. Di, B. H. May, A. L.
       Zhang, et al. "A Meta-analysis of Ear-Acupuncture, Ear-
       Acupressure and Auriculotherapy for Cigarette Smoking
       Cessation," *Drug Alcohol Dependency* 142 (Sept. 1, 2014):
       14–23.doi: 10.1016/j.drugalcdep.2014.07.002. Epub July 1,
       2014.

169   *"Healing therapies utilizing touch":* Rachel S. C. Friedman,
       Matthew M. Burg, Pamela Miles, Forrester Lee, and Rachel

Lampert, "Effects of Reiki on Autonomic Activity Early After Acute Coronary Syndrome," *Journal of American College of Cardiology* 56 (2010): 995–96, doi:10.1016/j.jacc.2010.03.082.

170   *"To keep the body":* Buddha quoted in Joey Klein, *The Inner Matrix: A Guide to Transforming Your Life and Awakening Your Spirit* (Bloomington, IN: Balboa Press, 2014), p. 136.

175   *"Exposure to these hormone disruptors":* National Institute of Environmental Health Sciences, website article titled "Endocrine Disruptors," http://www.niehs.nih.gov/health/topics/agents/endocrine/.

Chapter 10: Thank

180   *"There are only two ways":* Albert Einstein quoted in David T. Dellinger, *From Yale to Jail: The Life Story of a Moral Dissenter* (New York: Pantheon, 1993), p. 418.

188   *"Be yourself":* Wilde quoted in Ralph Keyes, *The Wit and Wisdom of Oscar Wilde* (New York: Gramercy Books, 1996).

190   *"studies have shown that happy people":* Hilary Tindle et al., "Optimism, Cynical Hostility, and Incident Coronary Heart Disease in the Women's Health Initiative," *Circulation* (Aug. 10, 2009), doi: 10.1161/CIRCULATIONAHA/108.827642.

190   *"Research shows that consistently grateful people":* Sonja Lyubomirsky, *The How of Happiness* (New York: Viking, 2008), p. 18.

190   *"In one study, a group of participants was asked":* J. K. Boehm, L. D. Kubzansky et al., "The Heart's Content: The Association Between Positive Psychological Well-being and Cardiovascular Health," *Psychological Bulletin*, 2012, psycnet.apa.org.

191 *"Severely depressed people who were told"*: Sonja Lyubomirsky and Nancy L. Sin, "Enhancing Well-Being and Alleviating Depressive Symptoms with Positive Psychology Interventions: A Practice-Friendly Meta-Analysis," *Journal of Clinical Psychology: In Session* 65 (5) (2009): 467–87, doi: 10.1002/jclp.20593. Published online in Wiley InterScience (www.interscience.wiley.com).

Chapter 11: Ground

196 *"The state of our health"*: Prince Charles, address to fifty-ninth World Health Assembly, http://bit.ly/1gdgiCd.

197 *"Emerging scientific research"*: G. Chevalier et al., "Earthing: Health Implications of Reconnecting the Human Body to the Earth's Surface Electrons," *Journal of Environmental Public Health* (2012), doi: 10.1155/2012/291541.

199 *"Besides BPA, substances"*: "Pollution in Minority Newborns: BPA and Other Cord Blood Pollutants," Environmental Working Group, Nov. 23, 2009, http://bit.ly/1KHETMa.

202 *spending time in nature . . . increased participants' energy:* Richard M. Ryan et al., "Vitalizing Effects of Being Outdoors and in Nature," *Journal of Environmental Psychology* 30, no. 2 (June 2010), pp. 159–68.

202 *participants were shown a traumatic video:* Roger Ulrich et al., "Stress Recovering During Exposure to Natural and Urban Environments," *Journal of Environmental Psychology* 11 (1991): 201–30.

203 *exercising outdoors improved participants' moods:* Peter Aspinall et al., "The Urban Brain: Analysing Outdoor Physical Activity with Mobile EEG," *British Journal of Sports Medicine* (June 2013), doi: 10.1136/bjsports-2012-091877.

203 *"one study discovered that children who were diagnosed with ADHD"*: A. F. Taylor and F. E. Kuo, "Children with

Attention Deficits Concentrate Better After Walk in the Park," *Journal of Attention Disorders* 12 no. 5 (March 2009): 402–9. doi: 10.1177/1087054708323000. Epub Aug. 25, 2008.

203 *moving to an area that has more green space:* Ian Alcock et al., "Longitudinal Effects on Mental Health of Moving to Greener and Less Green Urban Areas," *Environmental Science and Technology*, 48, no. 2 (2014): 1247–55, doi 10.1021/es403688w.

203 *nature increases your sense of awe:* Michelle N. Shiota and Dacher Keltner, "The Nature of Awe: Elicitors, Appraisals, and Effects on Self-Concept," *Cognition and Emotion* 21, no. 5 (2007): 944–63.

204 *"research has also shown that people who experience awe":* Paul K. Piff, Pia Dietze, Matthew Feinberg, et al., "Awe, the Small Self, and Prosocial Behavior," *Journal of Personality and Social Psychology*, 108 no. 6 (June 2015): 883–99. http://dx.doi .org/10.1037/pspi0000018.

204 *living near areas with walkable green spaces:* T. Takano, K. Nakamura, M. Watanabe, "Urban Residential Environments and Senior Citizens' Longevity in Megacity Areas: The Importance of Walkable Green Spaces," *Journal of Epidemiology and Community Health* 56, no. 12 (2002): 913–18, doi:10.1136/jech.56.12.913.

204 *individuals who were put in rooms with plants:* Seong-Hyun Park and Richard H. Mattson, "Effects of Flowering and Foliage Plants in Hospital Rooms on Patients Recovering from Abdominal Surgery," *HortTechnology* 18, no. 4 (2008): 563–68.

Acupuncture, 165, 167–169
ADHD (attention deficit/
    hyperactivity disorder), 203
Aerobics, 23
Affirmations, 111
Albom, Mitch, 212
Alcohol, 11, 17–19, 118–119
Alternative treatments, 166–170
Anderson, Carver, 99
Angina, 167–168
Animal House (movie), 62, 121
Antibiotics, 14, 161, 163, 174
Arrhythmia, 168
Arrien, Angeles, 192
Ashtanga yoga, 27
Ashwagandha, 173
Astrology, 112
Axelrod, David, 47

Back pain, 24–25, 29–32, 42, 162,
    171
Barefoot walking, 197–198
Beattie, Melody, 184
Being the Best (Waitley), 98

Believing, principle of, 6, 61–62,
    77–79, 83
Benson, Herbert, 32
Bike riding, 29
Bloating, 16, 174
Blood pressure, 167, 168, 170, 204
Blood testing, 172–173
Blue-Eyed Devil (Kleypas), 140
Branson, Richard, 54
Breathing, 6, 102–115
Brosnan, Pierce, 141
Buddha, 170
Budig, Kathryn, 4, 26, 32–33
Burbn, 55

Caddyshack (movie), 86
Caffeine, 16, 17, 203
Cahill, Kevin, 160–161
Cancer, 13, 168
"Cancer Loves Sugar" (*60 Minutes*),
    13
Career choice, 44–45, 51–55
Carr, Kris, 13
Carrey, Jim, 77

Index

Centre for Ageing Studies, Flinders University, Australia, 117

Chakras and Their Archetypes, 29–30

Chance opportunities, maximizing, 96–97

Charles, Prince, 196

Cheating, 120

Chemicals, 5, 14, 175, 196, 199–201, 206

Chewing food, 17

Chutkan, Robynne, 164, 166

Claudat, Dana, 106

Coconut oil, 18

Coffee, 10

Colbert, Stephen, 216

Colon hydrotherapy, 163

Communication, 149–150

Comparisons, 187–188, 193

Complete blood count, 173

Conduct of Life (Emerson), 4

Congestive heart failure, 168

Connecting the dots, 62–70, 74–75, 83

Connection, The (documentary), 31–32

Constipation, 16, 174

Corn, 19, 176

Cortisol, 170

Criticism, 151, 152

Cross, Joe, 99–100

Cross-Fit, 23

Crummy Brothers Organic Cookies, 23–24

Csikszentmihalyi, Mihaly, 50

Cupping, 165

Cytokines, 204

Dairy products, 18, 176

Dancing, 29

David and Goliath (Gladwell), 72

Death, 5, 6, 71, 209–222

Depression, 17, 43, 165, 191

Derderian, John, 124, 148

Dickens, Charles, 69

Diet and nutrition, 6, 8–21, 28, 78, 196

  alcohol, 11, 17–19, 118–119

  balance in, 15

  caffeine, 16, 17

  chewing food, 17

  dairy products, 18, 176

  diets, 9, 14

  digestion and, 16–17

  eating slowly, 20–21

  elimination diet, 19

  experimentation and, 20

  fats, 17

  fiber, 17

  food intolerances and sensitivities, 163, 174, 176

  food journal, 19

  food preservatives, 176

  fruit and vegetables, 14, 16

  gluten, 11, 13–15, 17–19, 166, 176

  juicing, 16, 159–160, 162–163

  junk food, 15

  meat, 11, 14, 165

  Paleo diet, 11, 164

  processed foods, 12–14, 175

  protein, 16, 17

Index

restaurant eating, 15
  skin issues and, 17–18
  soda, 12, 17
  sugar, 12–19, 166
Digestion, 16–17, 162
Doctors, choice of, 170–172,
  177
Dots, connecting, 62–70, 74–75,
  83
Doubt, 100
Doughnuts, 15
DuFresne, Aimee, 218–221
Dunbar, Robin, 118
Dyer, Wayne, 89
Dylan, Bob, 90

Eastern medicine, 161, 162,
  164–166
Eating (*see* Diet and nutrition)
Eating slowly, 20–21
Edison, Thomas, 162
Education through Recreation
  (Jacks), 89–90
Einstein, Albert, 179
Elimination diet, 19
Eliot, T. S., 55
Ellis, Albert, 128
Emerson, F. L., 78
Emerson, Ralph Waldo, 4
Emotional health, 6, 116–135
Endorphins, 202
Energy, types of, 126–127
Environment, 5, 6, 195–198,
  201–205
Environmental Working Group
  (EWG), 199–201, 206

Exercise, 6, 10–11, 22–34, 202–
  203
Exploration, 6, 84–101

Faith, 71–72, 74, 83
Fat Sick & Nearly Dead
  (documentary), 99–100
Fatigue, 16
Fats, 17
Fed Up (documentary), 12
Feelings (*see* Emotional health)
Fermented foods, 18
Ferris Bueller's Day Off (movie),
  226
Ferriss, Tim, 34
Fiber, 17
Fish oil, 173
Flow, finding, 49–51, 59
*Folks, This Ain't Normal: A Farmer's
  Advice for Happier Hens,
  Healthier People, and a Better
  World* (Salatin), 15
Food (*see* Diet and nutrition)
Food and Drug Administration
  (FDA), 13
Food journal, 19
Force of Nature (Hamilton), 198
Four Agreements, The (Ruiz), 142
4-Hour Body, The (Ferriss), 34
Frank, Anne, 205
Frankl, Viktor, 30
Fred (uncle), 38–40
Friendships, 6, 117–118, 122–127,
  133
Fruit, 14, 16
Functional medicine, 165–166

Game, The (Strauss), 148

Gandhi, Mahatma, 24

Garlic, 18

Gas, 16

Geffen, David, 48

Give and Take (Grant), 189

Givens, Raylan, 127

Gladwell, Malcolm, 53, 72, 118

Glenister, Tim, 99

Gluten, 11, 13–15, 17–19, 166, 176

Godwinks, 72, 74

Grains, 11

Grandmother, 37, 93, 94, 109, 131, 180, 209, 215–216

Grant, Adam, 189

Grass-fed meat, 14

Gratitude, 6, 176, 178–193, 196, 216

Gratitude journal, 191–193

Gretzky, Wayne, 97

Grief, 6, 71, 73, 212–222

Grounding, 6, 197–198, 205

Gut feelings, 129–132, 135

Gut flora, 17

Gut (microbiome), 43, 161–162, 164, 174, 177

Gutbliss (Chutkan), 164

Hahn, Scott MacKinlay, 56–58

Hamilton, Laird, 198

Harris, Dan, 47, 103–104

Harvey, Shannon, 31–32

Hay, Louise, 111–112

Health, 6, 10, 80–83, 158–177

Heart disease, 13, 168, 170

Heart health, 167–170

Heartland Securities, 67–68

Herophilus, 159

High-fructose corn syrup, 12

High-intensity interval training (HIIT), 23

Hill, Armond, 127

Hill, Napoleon, 40

Hodgson, Rob, 182

How of Happiness, The (Lyubomirsky), 190, 191

"Hunted Down" (Dickens), 69

Hyman, Mark, 13, 165

Hypertension, 168

Immune system, 18, 203–204

In Defense of Food (Pollan), 14

Indigestion, 16

Indoor plants, 204–205

Inflammation markers, 176, 204

Instagram, 55–56

Instincts, 97, 129–132, 135

International Orange, San Francisco, 29

Irritability, 17

Irritable bowel syndrome (IBS), 16

Iyengar, B. K. S., 26

Jacks, Lawrence Pearsall, 89–91, 95

Jobs, 5, 6, 36–59

Jobs, Steve, 54, 56, 62, 69

Jogging, 23, 29, 32

Johnson, Sue, 4, 150–155

Juicing, 16, 159–160, 162–163

Junk food, 15

Justified (Givens), 127

Index

Kabat-Zinn, Jon, 103
Kahn, Joel, 166–170
Katie, Byron, 215
Keep Going: From Grief to Growth
  (DuFresne), 218–221
Keller, Helen, 45
Kleypas, Lisa, 140
Knoles, Charlie, 4, 113–115
Kondo, Marie, 107
Kotler, Steven, 50–51
Kresser, Chris, 11

Lancet, 117
Language of Letting Go, The
  (Beattie), 183
Laughter, 6, 216, 217, 224–227
Learned Optimism (Seligman),
  128–129
Lee, Bruce, 46
Legs Up the Wall pose, 33
Lewis, C. S., 92, 95
Lewis, Michael, 64
Liar's Poker (Lewis), 64
Life-Changing Magic of Tidying Up
  (Kondo), 107
LinkedIn, 53
Lipid panel, 173
Lipman, Frank, 4, 16, 160, 161,
  163, 165
Living, mastering art of, 89–90,
  101
Long Walk to Freedom (Mandela),
  99
Longfellow, Henry Wadsworth, 72
Loomstate, 56
Love, defined, 146–147

Loving What Is (Katie), 215
Low-carb diet, 11, 93
Low-sugar diet, 11
Luck Factor, The (Wiseman), 96
Luckiness, concept of, 96–97, 100
Lyubomirsky, Sonja, 190, 191

Maher, Bill, 12
Mandela, Nelson, 99
Man's Search for Meaning (Frankl),
  30
Massage therapy, 167, 170, 177
McCarthy, Cormac, 80
Meat, 11, 14, 165
Meditation, 11, 46, 103–106,
  113–115, 159, 166, 170, 173,
  196
Mere Christianity (Lewis), 92
Metabolism, 162
Microbiome, 43, 161–162, 164,
  174, 177
Midsummer Night's Dream, A
  (Shakespeare), 144
Milliken, Austin, 148
Mind-body connection, 5, 103,
  107–108, 111, 115, 195
Mind Over Medicine (Rankin), 107
mindbodygreen, 4, 5, 31, 47, 52,
  69, 77–78, 95–96, 99, 112,
  122–124, 195, 197
Mindfulness, 15, 133
Mindfulness meditation, 104–105
Moehringer, J. R., 118–119
Monroe, Marilyn, 70
Mourning, 71, 73, 212–222
Move (*see* Exercise)

Muir, John, 197
Mullen, Seamus, 165

Namath, Joe, 73
Nature, 5, 6, 195–198, 201–205
New Age perspective, 30, 46
Newborn umbilical blood cord
    samples, 199
9/11 terrorist attacks, 73, 130–131,
    159
No Country for Old Men
    (McCarthy), 80
No More Dirty Looks (O'Connor
    and Spunt), 200
Nutrition (*see* Diet and nutrition)
Nuts, 16, 176

Obesity, 13
O'Connor, Siobhan, 200
O'Loughlin, Kathy, 214
O'Loughlin, Tim, 213–214,
    216–217
Optimism, 61–62, 128–129
Ornish, Dean, 32
Orthorexia, 12
Osteen, Joel, 71
Our National Parks (Muir), 197
Outliers (Gladwell), 118

Paleo diet, 11, 164
Parasites, 160–161, 163–164
Paul, Sheryl, 132–135
Peale, Norman Vincent, 85
Peer pressure, 121
Pessimism, 128–129
Pesticides, 175

Phosphatidylserine, 173
Picoult, Jodi, 110
Plastics, 175
Platonic love, 137, 143, 147–148,
    156
Player, Gary, 41–42
Pollan, Michael, 14
Power of Positive Thinking, The
    (Peale), 85
Pressfield, Steven, 43
Probiotics, 18, 161, 174
Processed foods, 12–14, 175
Protein, 16, 17
*Psychology of Optimal Experience,
    The* (Csikszentmihalyi), 50
Pulse, resting, 174

Rankin, Lissa, 107, 190
Raw foods, 11
Reiki, 165, 167, 169
Relationships, 6, 136–156
Remen, Rachel Naomi, 192
Rescue, The (Sparks), 146
Resistance training, 23
Restaurant eating, 15
Resting pulse, 174
Rhodolia, 173
Rice, Condoleezza, 71
Robbins, Tony, 37
Rohan, Jack, 225
Roll, Rich, 29
Romantic love, 137, 147, 150,
    153–156
Romm, Aviva, 80–83
Roosevelt, Theodore, 61
Root chakra, 30

Index

Ruiz, Don Miguel, 142
Rushnell, SQuire, 72

Salatin, Joel, 15
Sandler, Adam, 73
Seat of the Soul, The (Zukav), 138
Seated Meditation, 33
Seeing, principle of, 79, 83
Seinfeld, Jerry, 94
Self-confidence, 78
Seligman, Martin, 128–129
Service industry, 86–88
Shadow of the Wind, The (Zafón), 86
Shah, Amy, 172–176
Shakespeare, William, 144
Shaw, George, 187
Shaw, Kerry, 123–124
Shiatsu, 165
"Should" statements, 132–135
Silver linings, 75–76
Silver Linings Playbook (movie), 75, 76
60 Minutes, 13
Skin issues, 17–18
Sleep, 43, 173
Smoking, 167, 168–169
Smoothies, 16
Social groups, 117–122, 135
Soda, 12, 17
Soul mates, 142–150, 156
Soy products, 19
Sparks, Nicholas, 146
Spunt, Alexandra, 200
Standing Forward Fold, 33–34
Stealing, 119–120, 184–185

Stiles, Tara, 26, 110, 123
Stonewalling, 151–152
Strala Yoga, New York, 26
Strauss, Neil, 148
Stress, 24, 32, 43, 58, 108, 111, 112, 149–150, 159, 165, 173, 175, 202, 210–211
Sugar, 12–19, 166
Sulfates, 176
Supine Twist, 33
Supplements, 173–174
Swimming, 29, 203

Tai Chi, 170
Taking action, principle of, 79, 83
Tao of Jeet Kune Do (Lee), 46
Taylor, Michael, 26, 110, 123
10% Happier (Harris), 47
Tender Bar, The (Moehringer), 118–119
Tenth Circle, The (Picoult), 110
Thanks (*see* Gratitude)
Therapeutic touch, 169–170
Thich Nhat Hanh, 105
Think and Grow Rich (Hill), 40
Thomas Crown Affair, The (movie), 141
Thompson, Patricia, 201–205
Thoreau, Henry David, 217
Three Question Journal, 192
Thyroid panel, 173
Tipping Point, The (Gladwell), 53
To Love This Life (Keller), 45
Transit of Venus (Hazzard), 55
Trust, 100
Tuesdays with Morrie (Albom), 212

Index

Tunney, Peter, 179
Type A personality, 45, 48

Unleash the Power Within
    (Robbins), 37

Vegetables, 14, 164
Vegetarianism, 11
Vinyasa flow, 26, 27
Visualization, 61, 77, 80–83
Vitamin C, 173
Vitamin D, 18
Volunteering, 188–189, 193

Wachob, Colleen, 5, 20, 28, 29, 32,
    51–52, 63, 99, 105, 108–112,
    123, 124, 144–146, 149, 160,
    171, 179, 187, 212
Wachob (father), 71, 73, 170, 180,
    181, 209–214, 216
Wachob (mother), 37–38, 94, 109,
    124–125, 130, 131, 170–171,
    180, 182, 183, 209, 210, 212,
    214, 215
Wahls, Terry, 164, 165
Waitley, Denis, 98
Walking, 29, 32, 34, 197–198

War of Art, The (Pressfield), 43
Weight lifting, 23
Weil, Andrew, 32
Western medicine, 161–166
Wherever You Go, There You Are
    (Kabat-Zinn), 103
Whey protein, 16
White, Heather, 200–201
Whole Foods Markets, 24
Wilde, Oscar, 188
Williams, Serena, 109
Winfrey, Oprah, 54, 176
Wiseman, Richard, 96
Wooden, John, 188
Work, 5, 6, 36–59

Yoga, 5, 10–11, 23, 25–30, 32–34,
    46, 113, 159, 162, 170, 171,
    173, 196
Yoga: The Path to Holistic Health
    (Iyengar), 26
You Can Heal Your Life (Hay),
    111–112

Zafón, Carlos Ruiz, 86
Zukav, Gary, 138

ABOUT THE AUTHOR

JASON WACHOB IS THE FOUNDER and CEO of mindbodygreen, the leading independent media brand dedicated to health and happiness, with 15 million monthly unique visitors. He has been featured in the *New York Times, Entrepreneur, Fast Company,* and *Vogue.* Jason has a BA in history from Columbia University, where he played varsity basketball for four years. He lives in Brooklyn with his wife, and he loves German shepherds, Chuck Taylors, and guacamole.

Follow Jason on Twitter and Instagram at @jasonwachob and visit wellth.mindbodygreen.com and share the #wellth.